MOMS ON THE JOB

Tyndale House Publishers, Inc., Carol Stream, Illinois

Moms on the job

7 SECRETS FOR SUCCESS AT HOME AND WORK

Sabrina O'Malone

Moms on the Job
Copyright © 2006 by Sabrina O'Malone
All rights reserved. International copyright secured.

ISBN-10: 1-58997-357-7
ISBN-13: 978-1-58997-357-2

A Focus on the Family book published by
Tyndale House Publishers, Carol Stream, Illinois 60188

TYNDALE is a registered trademark of Tyndale House Publishers, Inc. Tyndale's quill
logo is a trademark of Tyndale House Publishers, Inc.

All Scripture quotations, unless otherwise indicated, are taken from *The Message*
(MSG) paraphrase. Copyright © 1993, 1994, 1995 by Eugene H. Peterson. Used by
permission of NavPress Publishing Group. Scripture quotations marked NIV are
taken from the *Holy Bible, New International Version®*. NIV®. Copyright © 1973,
1978, 1984 by International Bible Society. Used by permission of Zondervan Publishing House. All rights reserved. Scripture quotations marked (NKJV) are taken from
the *New King James Version*. Copyright © 1982 by Thomas Nelson, Inc. Used by
permission. All rights reserved.

The names of some of the persons whose stories are told in this book have been
changed to protect their privacy.

Editor: Kathy Davis
Cover design by Jennifer Lund
Cover photo © by On Request. All rights reserved.

Library of Congress Cataloging-in-Publication Data
O'Malone, Sabrina, date
Moms on the job : 7 secrets for success at home and work / Sabrina O'Malone.
   p. cm.
"A Focus on the Family book."
ISBN-13: 978-1-58997-357-2
ISBN-10: 1-58997-357-7
1. Working mothers—Religious life. I. Title.
BV4529.18.O53 2006
248.8'431—dc22
                                                      2005032246

Printed in the United States of America
1 2 3 4 5 6 7 8 9 / 12 11 10 09 08 07 06

This book is dedicated to those who came before me:

Stormie Omartian—Thank you for showing me how to love my God, my husband, and my children—all at the same time.

John C. Maxwell—Your encouragement has meant the world to me. When I grow up, I want to be like you . . . but a woman.

Thelma Wells—The Lord has used you greatly to encourage and inspire millions. You are the Heart to Heart Encourager, and a faithful friend.

Hattie Ridley—My great-grandmother, the first Negro woman to own and operate an American plantation. We have not forgotten where we came from, and we teach it to our children.

Contents

Foreword ix

Introduction 1

Prologue—The Typical Morning 3

Secret 1—Find Prayer Partners 9

Secret 2—Eliminate the Extraneous 19

Secret 3—Start Delegating 35

Secret 4—Learn to Multitask 55

Secret 5—Show Up Big Time 63

Secret 6—Set Goals for Success 77

Secret 7—Replenish Your Body, Mind, and Spirit 87

Epilogue—The New Typical Morning 101

Appendix 1: Making the Decision to Work Outside
     the Home 105

Appendix 2: Great Time-Savers for Families 107

Acknowledgments 113

Foreword

I read the book last Friday and loved it. From Sabrina's firsthand experience as a working mom in the corporate arena, raising three children, being a wife to Daniel, and a homemaker at the same time, she speaks straight from the horse's—Oh! I don't mean horse's—I mean from the overwhelmed mom's mouth. Well, she used to be overwhelmed until she started *living* her life instead of letting life live her.

The pages of *Moms on the Job* are saturated with the cooling water of Scripture and prayer. Time with God is not the last resort to a working mom; it is the first consideration of each day. Beginning the day with God is like resting in a warm bath with your favorite fragrance of bath oil . . . rejuvenating.

Girl, if I had been privileged to read this when I was a working mom raising three kids and a husband, it would not have taken me until I became a grandmother to understand some of the insights in this life-changing book.

I'm giving a copy of this book to my daughters, friends, and acquaintances. I'm positive that when they read it and apply it, their homes will become sanctuaries of order, peace, controlled living, and greater financial stability. Owning this book is a must for every household.

Even if you are not a mom or a working mom, you can benefit by the strategies and words of admonition that fit you. The weight loss one hit me square in the eyes. What a gift to women everywhere!

—Thelma Wells
Key Speaker, Women of Faith®

Introduction

"Hey, you look familiar! Don't we know each other?" A young woman with a three year old in tow stopped me in the grocery store.

"I was thinking the same thing," I replied. "Don't you work for a pharmaceutical company?"

"Yes, I do," she answered.

"What a beautiful little girl you have." I tousled her daughter's golden locks. "And how have you been?" I asked, redirecting my attention to the mother.

"I'm hanging in there," she responded. "I took the day off to catch up on some paperwork and spend a little extra time with her."

It was already 5:30 P.M. and she was still grocery shopping. *She'll be lucky to get dinner ready before 7:00*, I thought. Her daughter popped open a bag of organic chips and began to eat them, as if she were reading my mind.

"You do the same kind of work I do . . . with more kids at home, yet you don't seem frazzled, and you look great. How do you do it?" Her eyes held the desperate longing for wisdom I've seen in the eyes of countless other working mothers.

Moms On the Job: 7 Secrets for Success at Home and Work was written to answer this heartfelt question: "How do you do it?" The short answer is, "With God's help and by keeping priorities in order." Of course, there's a longer answer, which I'll share with you in this book.

There are two types of working moms: those who are enjoying it, and those who are not. Some women would rather be at home full-time, while others prefer working to staying at home. But many working moms have crunched the numbers and they simply must work—whether they would prefer to or not. Regardless of where you are on this continuum, *Moms on the Job* was written to address the nuts and bolts of how to juggle work and family—while keeping your family your top priority.

So how can you be a competent, dependable employee while providing for and doing what's best for your children? Read on; this book is for you! (And if you're rethinking your decision to be in the workforce or you're considering returning to the workplace after a time at home, please see Appendix 1: "Making the Decision to Work Outside the Home.")

It is my hope and prayer that this book will encourage, inspire, and revitalize the busiest people in the world today—the 36 million mothers in America's paid labor force, two out of three of whom are full-time.

You've paid your dues. You've worked hard enough. It's high time someone let you in on the secrets to phenomenal success. Welcome to the club. Sit back, relax, and get ready to be amazed.

The Typical Morning

6:15 A.M.—The beeping alarm clock startles you into reality. It's time to get going. You press snooze.

6:24—Alarm beeps again, but you still have plenty of time. You hit the easiest button—the big wide snooze, of course.

6:33—*Beep-beep.* So tired . . . so sleepy . . . so justified. You press the snooze button again.

6:42—*Beep-beep-beep!* With a sigh you hit snooze, this time determined to mentally plan out everything you need to do: *Get up, put in contacts, put on beige outfit, find knee-highs in the laundry basket . . .* as you drift off contentedly to slumber.

6:51—*BEEP-BEEP-BEEP!* Now the situation is serious. You crawl out of bed, quietly praying the kids won't wake up and slow down the process of getting the day started.

7:00—By the time you find your other matching sock, you realize you have no time for a shower and you will have to put on your makeup in the car. You let the dog out.

7:15—First child wakes up.
- Lunches aren't prepared.
- You haven't had a quiet time.
- Even cereal for breakfast would be a luxury.

7:30—One child is dressed and drinking milk while parked in front of the TV. You feed the dog and begin to make lunches.

7:45—Next child awakens. Frantically, you pick out what you hope is "all-purpose clothing" because you haven't a clue about the weather. With a peek out the window you conclude that sweats will be fine.

7:48—Child argues. Does not *want* to wear the outfit. Your temper begins to rise as you insist that she *will.*

7:49—Child #1 gets bored with TV and requests a grilled cheese sandwich for breakfast.

It's 8:00!—You run the mental checklist:
- Any field trip or other permission slips needed today?
- School fund-raisers due?
- Is it show-and-tell day?
- Are library books due?

8:03—The bus rolls up. Shouting for jackets, caps, and lunchboxes, you propel the kids out the door with a piece of toast and a kiss.

8:05—Now you calculate everything you'll need for work.

8:10—While driving to work you realize:
- You didn't take meat out of the freezer to thaw for dinner.
- You never called your mother back.
- The sink is full of dishes.

• Your husband is down to his last pair of clean underwear.

You pray God will get you through this day.

8:30 A.M.—After applying makeup haphazardly in the car, you walk into the workplace feeling like you've already put in a day's work . . . and you haven't even gotten started.

To be honest, this was a pretty smooth morning. The bus wasn't late, none of the kids were sick, the family dog didn't dart out the door, and no one needed extra cuddle time. To top it off, you made it in to work on time—with your makeup on!

Have I gotten your attention? Does this typical morning scenario sound awfully familiar? Chances are it does! Don't despair; God is waiting to intervene in every difficult morning of your life. Let's invite Him in with prayer.

❈ PRAYER

Lord,

I lay all my responsibilities at Your feet. I am now yielding my heart, mind, and strength to Your awesome power and glory. I desperately need You.

Open my eyes, ears, heart, and soul so I'm not too busy to hear You. Teach me to walk, live, and be in the center of Your will for my life. Use me as a blessing in the lives of my children, dear Lord.

Forgive me for my past mistakes, which can be better described as sins. I've been impatient, short-tempered, and self-righteous, and it has made me a difficult woman to love and live with. Lord, starting today, fill me with the

fruit of the Spirit: love, joy, peace, patience, kindness, good-
ness, faithfulness, gentleness, and self-control.
  Make me a woman who is not easily angered; guard
me from being rude or selfish. Fill me with the strength to
endure all things necessary. Your perfect love never fails. I
praise You, and I thank You for saving me.
  Amen.

❃ FAITH IN ACTION

Circle the three things below that cause you the most distress.

Fatigue	Worry about work
Stress	Being behind in housework
Anxiety about your kids	Lack of finances
Loneliness	Angry outbursts
Lack of hope	Discouragement

Fill in the blanks below with your circled words.

Lord, I hereby release my _____,
_____, *and my* _____
to You. It is entirely up to You to handle them.

Circle the three corresponding opposites of your list above.

Energy	Fulfillment
Peace	Well-run household
Trust and confidence	Abundance
Companionship	Words of blessing
Optimism	Encouragement

Now fill in the blanks with your newly circled replacements.

Lord, I hereby charge You with the task of filling my life with

_____, _____,

and _____. *With Your help, I will
be like clay being molded into something beautiful, purposeful, and
deliberately designed by You, the Master.*

    Amen

Signed_____

Date_____

Find Prayer Partners

I have one request, dear friends: Pray for me.
Pray strenuously with and for me—to God the Father,
through the power of our Master Jesus,
through the love of the Spirit.
—ROMANS 15:30

I know what it's like to walk through the valley of the shadow of death—with my unborn child. I was three months pregnant, and was scheduled to have a grapefruit-sized tumor removed because it was threatening the pregnancy.

Frankly, I was petrified, knowing how rare surgery is on a pregnant woman because of the risks to both the mother and child. I cried out to God, my husband, friends, and relatives. Desperate for a miracle, I turned to the church for prayer. It was then that I began to see the church as something more than a building where people go to talk about Jesus.

Many dear women sought me out, called me, sent cards, and encouraged me in a very tangible way by bringing food to my family. Each one of them let me know she was praying for us. Although most of these women were members of our local church, many of them were believers from different denominations. I was humbled by the overwhelming love and grace lived out before my eyes.

The morning of the surgery, I prayed like never before for my child. A great big wordless plea of a mother's heart went up before the throne room of God. That's all I could pray before I went under.

I awoke in the recovery room, barely able to utter the question, "My baby?"

The operating room nurse looked directly into my eyes, took me by the hand, and said, "Sabrina, your baby is fine. Would you like to hear the heartbeat?"

The swishing sound of my baby's heartbeat was like a chorus of angels testifying to God's mercy. I was awed by such amazing grace. My husband and I were not alone in our joy as the entire Presbyterian church in New Brunswick, New Jersey, rejoiced with us.

I suspect that God would still have blessed us even if the church had not supported us in prayer. But there is an undeniable value in being able to share the blessings of answered prayer with a group who prays for you and with you.

When my son, Daniel, was christened, every heart was moved. There were many tears of joy as everyone remembered their own private and collective prayers for this precious little child.

Several women emerged out of this crisis to become my greatest mentors and prayer partners. Most of them are middle-aged, but one lady is 96 and another is a teenager. They are different nationalities, some are married, others are widows, some are single, and others are stay-at-home mothers. Matthew 18:20 says, "And when two or three of you are together because of me, you can be sure that I'll be there."

Prayer is the key to opening joy, gratitude, praise, and fulfillment to you, especially when other people support you in prayer.

You will have the presence and power of God's Holy Spirit in and throughout your life. This is the Lord's promise to you.

I can almost hear the questions: "Sabrina, what are you saying? How will this make it easier to get through the day? What does this have to do with being a working mom?" I'll explain by giving you another example from my own life.

PRAYER PARTNERS AND MARRIAGE

On top of another very difficult pregnancy, I had two major surgeries in the months following the birth of our second child, Christiana. When I returned to work full-time, I quickly became overwhelmed as I tried to manage our household and meet the needs of two young children and my husband. From sunup until well past sundown I was seriously busy. There was *always* something important I couldn't quite make the time for.

It wasn't long before I began to resent my husband's laid-back demeanor. This was a big change, because his calmness and level-headedness had formerly been characteristics I found refreshing. Once the comparisons began, score was kept. Our new favorite word became "I." Our marriage was in a downward spiral, and we both knew it.

In desperation I purchased several Christian books on marriage, and they all instructed, "Get your prayer partners to pray for you." There was only one problem: I didn't *have* any prayer partners. Still, I was willing to try anything, so with the Lord's help, I asked several women in my church to pray for my marriage—without giving them a whole lot of details.

Each of them said she would be happy to do it. Then I began to pray for my husband. Dan and I instituted a weekly date night and attended a "Family Life" marriage conference, all while being lifted up in prayer by others.

The changes between us were nothing less than dramatic. Our marriage began to show new life within the first few days. Over the next few months, things continued to improve even more. I am happy to report that today we are even more in love and more of a team than when we first married. I attribute these changes to God's grace and the impact of prayer.

THE VALUE OF MENTORS

Mentors are absolutely vital for a working mother. A mentoring relationship can be described like this: Picture yourself as a small, tired child. (This should be easy for any working mother.) Now, envision yourself climbing into the lap of a loving mother. Imagine yourself being rocked and comforted while she gently strokes your hair. After a meaningful conversation with a mentor, you will feel as secure as this child. Working mothers desperately need relationships from which they can receive wisdom, love, and nurturing. It is available to you if you'll begin by asking a few trustworthy women to pray for you. Then ask the Lord to develop these relationships into mentoring relationships.

The Bible encourages women of all ages to maintain relationships with one another (see Titus 2:3-5). But asking someone else to pray for your particular situation can be intimidating. Thus, it's important that you carefully and prayerfully select your prayer partners based on their characters and maturity. Remember, maturity isn't necessarily about age. Some younger women are more spiritually mature than many older women. The idea is to select women who are not given to gossip and who love the Lord.

I cannot emphasize strongly enough that you select *only* women as intimate prayer partners. Just imagine all the potential areas of temptation involved with sharing your innermost thoughts, challenges, and feelings with someone of the opposite sex. Unless that man is your husband, reaching this degree of emotional intimacy is a red flag signaling danger! Most affairs begin with some kind of emotional "connection," and those who assume they are above temptation are in the most danger. But even if you would never entertain the thought, a male "good friend" might. And thoughts like this can—and will—take away from the original purpose, which is prayer for you about a specific challenge or struggle.

Finding the Right Prayer Partners for You

Proverbs 31:25-26 describes a godly woman like this: "Her clothes are well-made and elegant, and she always faces tomorrow with a smile. When she speaks she has something worthwhile to say, and she always says it kindly." A similar passage is in Titus 2:3: "Guide older women into lives of reverence so they end up as neither gossips nor drunks, but models of goodness. By looking at them, the younger women will know how to love their husbands and children, be virtuous and pure, keep a good house, be good wives."

Can you think of a woman who is elegant and faces life with a smile? Can you think of an older woman who is reverent, a woman whom you've never heard say a bad thing about anyone? If so, she would probably be honored to hear you tell her she reminds you of a Titus woman. This is the type of woman you could trust to commit any situation of yours to prayer.

If you don't know of any women like this within your circle of acquaintances, don't worry. God does. He's got you covered by His loving-kindness and has made a provision for you: It's called the church. Ask your pastor to recommend some women who would fit the description of a godly woman given in Proverbs and Titus.

Did She Say the Church?

Yes, I did. However, I cannot ignore the sincerity and devotion I've seen in the lives of many of my nonchurchgoing friends. I wrote this book to benefit *all* working moms, and yes, it's based on a Judeo-Christian perspective. Why? The bottom line is this: Successfully giving 100 percent to your children and 100 percent on the job requires you to give 200 percent, day after day, year after year. And you're going to need a miracle to pull it off. Anyone who tells you different is selling something. Fortunately, God is in the business of miracles.

If you've encountered people who have given you a bad impression of Christians as a whole, I sincerely hope and pray that I will reflect God's love, grace, and compassion to you. Developing your relationship with God is the most important proven secret to success. The Lord's supernatural touch is available and always just a prayer away.

The stories in this book are about real women who have experienced God's miraculous grace through the power of prayer and who have been kind enough to give me permission to share God's miracles in their lives. It's my prayer that you will be as encouraged and uplifted by their stories as I have been.

PRAYER PARTNERS AND CHILDREN

The story of Daphne beautifully illustrates how collective prayer and having prayer partners and mentors can enrich the life of a working mother. She became a believer at the age of 18. As is the case with most 18-year-old women, she anxiously looked forward to marriage in her future. Thirteen years later, the Lord sent her Ron, a godly man whom she adored and married within a year.

A few years into Daphne and Ron's marriage, there were still no children. If you or any of your friends have ever struggled with infertility, you know how this can steal your joyful countenance.

After praying for over a year on their own, Daphne and Ron enlisted the prayer support of their church. Daphne already had some Christian women in her life she considered friends, but when she asked them to pray for her about such an important struggle, those relationships deepened. Her Christian friends became her prayer partners, and her prayer partners became mentors.

One January morning, while praying in her car about her husband's health, she heard the Lord saying, "I have heard your prayers and will give you the desires of your heart. Your husband's diabetes will be under control, and I will bless you with children." She was greatly encouraged, as you can imagine.

After many years of waiting and trying, Daphne gave birth on Father's Day to a son they named Jacob. (Ron said this gift surely topped the leaf blower she bought him the year before.)

PRAYER PARTNERS AND HEALTH

Sara is a woman who knows about powerful and effective prayer. She has heard the three words no one wants to hear from her doctor: "You have cancer."

Sara, a mother of two daughters, was working full time as a medical practice administrator when she received the diagnosis. After sharing the news with her family, one of her daughters asked, "When are you going to die from this, Mom?"

This heartfelt, naïve question ignited sparks of faith within Sara. Possessing the peace that surpasses understanding in regard to her cancer, she believed in her heart it would not take her life. Although she previously had not been very religious, she invited her relatives to come to her home on the night before her surgery to pray with her.

As a matter of course, she sent out an internal e-mail at her job, letting her coworkers know of her upcoming surgery. Sara closed the e-mail welcoming their well wishes, thoughts, and prayers, and mentioned her plans for her family gathering on the night before her surgery.

Unbeknownst to Sara, one of her coworkers forwarded the e-mail to her mother, who forwarded it to a local church. Another coworker forwarded the e-mail to her sister in Germany. Sara's prayer request quickly traveled all over the world.

The night before her surgery, a small group of Sara's relatives assembled in her home. Even her father (who wasn't a believer) came. When they began to pray, a white light and an overwhelming sense of peace came down and surrounded the circle. All those who were present burst into tears! This manifestation of the Holy Spirit moved even the hardest of hearts.

When Sara went in for her surgery the next morning, there was no cancer to be found. And it hasn't returned in three years!

Expressions like "Rejoice, be glad, praise and give thanks" hardly seem adequate when God performs a miracle. Even if you have yet to experience or recognize God's miraculous handiwork in your own life, pray and praise the Lord with me right now.

❈ PRAYER

Lord,

Thank You for Your promise to supply all of my needs. Thank You for the countless times You've protected me and blessed me, especially those times when I never knew You were there.

The Bible says You are always with me; You'll never leave me or forsake me. This is the kind of love I've longed for my entire life. With all power and strength in Your hands, You know me completely, and love me still. You provide for me and protect me. You even gave up Your life to save mine.

Help me to know I can do all things in Your strength. Having prayer partners and mentors sounds wonderful. As I lay my needs before You, I pray for Your strength. Make me bold enough to ask a few other women to pray for my family and for me.

Put the right godly women in my life, Lord. Guard my heart, thoughts, and actions from things displeasing to You. Keep me from evil. I pray without ceasing for Your abundant blessing on my family. Mold us into exactly what You would have us to be. Use me as an instrument of Your divine will.

Amen.

❀ FAITH IN ACTION

List the names of several women you can ask to pray for you.

Write down what you would like them to pray about for you.

Pray for these women right now, asking God to bless them, their families, and their walk with Him.

✺ BETWEEN FRIENDS

1. Have you ever experienced or do you know someone who has experienced a miracle?

2. How would witnessing a miracle change you? Would your faith be radically different?

3. What do you believe most hinders your experience with miraculous events?

Eliminate the Extraneous

Looking at it one way, you could say, "Anything goes.
Because of God's immense generosity and grace, we
don't have to dissect and scrutinize every action to see if
it will pass muster." But the point is not to just get by.
—1 CORINTHIANS 10:23

As a working mother, you've probably noticed you are often pressed for time. Your time is valuable to God, your family, your employer, and to you. This is exactly why you must consciously decide what things are beneficial and constructive and invest your time in those things.

If you feel overwhelmed, then it is time to take stock of your commitments and examine how you spend your time off the clock. It may be possible you don't need to be such an integral member of all the worthy causes you are currently committed to—at least for now.

YOUR LIFE, YOUR GARDEN

Enid, a busy mother of five children, shared this analogy with me:
A young woman decided to take up gardening as a hobby.

She purchased everything she needed, including a how-to manual about the subject. She set out with vigor to create her garden.

She selected a location with the right amount of sunlight and shade, the right kind of topsoil, and she even meticulously measured the depth, width, and spacing required. She planted her garden, and soon the little seedlings appeared. She was overjoyed! She could already envision the fruit that would someday be hers.

She read on in the manual, and to her dismay the book instructed her to pull out every other seedling! She read it twice to be certain. Her mind was filled with questions. *Does this apply to my particular garden?* She went out and examined her creation.

Each precious plant was growing beautifully, and to her eye, it seemed obvious they had plenty of space and room to continue to do so. There was nothing wrong with any of them.

Perhaps, she thought, *the instructions apply to other gardeners who are growing something else. My garden is doing well, and I've already promised to give the fruit to people who really need it. I simply can't cut this crop in half!* She did not have the heart to pull up any of the seedlings. So they all continued to grow . . . for a while.

Any experienced gardener can tell you the folly of this decision. Though things looked great aboveground, underneath, the roots became so entangled and tight that no plant could reach its full potential. Ultimately, none of her plants bore any fruit.

How does this apply to moms? Those beautiful, healthy seedlings are like the many opportunities that come our way—opportunities that look so good and healthy. There is nothing inherently wrong with joining the PTA or being a Scout leader, belonging to an auxiliary club or serving on the school board. Nor is there anything wrong with a few extracurricular activities for your children—be it soccer, football, ballet lessons, karate, piano lessons, or cheerleading. These are all good things.

The problem arises when activities keep the family in constant motion, struggling to keep up with a hectic schedule. Like the little seedlings crowding out each other, the carpooling and errands associated with extracurricular activities may be choking the life out of your family.

It can be hard to let go of something good, especially when it's just to make room for "free time." The temporary anguish associated with cutting back, however, is worth the long-term joy of experiencing a peaceful, less-hectic family life. Pray about which of your own painstakingly planted "seedlings" need to be pulled out. Ask the Lord where He would have your family expend its time and energy. I am already praying with you.

Feeding without Getting Fed

All of us need to carefully consider where God is really calling us to serve, but especially those of us who are employed in the paid workforce. It's such a temptation to want to take on the noble calling of church work. But overcommitment to even the church may not be where God is calling you to serve right now.

The following story illustrates perfectly the temptation to go all out in the name of really, really being of service to God and others. Can you imagine the joyous anticipation you would feel if 15 of the most recognizable leaders in Christianity decided to have dinner and fellowship at your home? One woman didn't have to imagine, because it happened to her.

Martha, blessed with the spiritual gift of hospitality, had a legitimate reason to put her best foot forward, for a very important person was coming to her house for lunch. She had to cook enough food for 15 or more people, create a place for them to sit, and apply the finishing touches that would make this a memorable experience. She wisely called her sister for help, as her hometown was out of the way of caterers and large supermarket chains. Everyone arrived together. What joy she felt to see her home so used by her special guests!

"What can I get you to drink?" she asked as her guests arrived.

"Just water, thank you."

"Me, too, I'm parched."

"That goes double for me!"

"I'll have a glass of wine—the red."

"Sounds good!"

"I'll take some of your white wine."

"I'd like some too."

Everyone seemed to answer simultaneously.

"I'll get those drinks while you all sit down and enjoy some fresh-baked bread and appetizers at the table." She was more grateful than ever to have her sister there to help.

After she poured the drinks, her work was just beginning; she still had to serve the food. Then she noticed her sister, just sitting there with the guests, listening with complete fascination to what was undoubtedly a great story.

Maybe it was nerves or stress, but the sight made her mad—so mad she chose to bring this situation before her special guest immediately. After all, there was more work than Martha and the servants could do. She needed all hands on deck! So she said to her VIP guest, "Don't you care that my sister has left me to do the work by myself? Tell her to help me!"

Frankly, I would have done the same thing. But she received an unexpected answer. "Martha, Martha, you are worried and upset about many things, but only one thing is needed. Mary has chosen what is better, and it will not be taken away from her."

You guessed it; this story comes from the Bible (Luke 10:38-42, NIV), and it's just as relevant today as it was when Jesus spoke those words to Martha. The Bible story of the sisters Mary and Martha serves to remind us that we're not expected to work so hard to serve God that we miss the opportunity to enjoy Him and listen to Him!

Here's some food for thought: The very same Jesus that Martha worked so hard to feed is the Man who fed 5,000 people with one little boy's lunch. It was Jesus who turned water into fine wine at a wedding celebration. Did He really need Martha to knock herself out to feed everyone? Does He really need you to serve on every committee that asks you?

If you feel pressed for time, minimizing or eliminating your nonessential involvements will free you up to take care of higher priority activities. Just being more relaxed and available to your family may be the higher priority the Lord has for you right now. Remember, if it is getting more and more difficult to keep up with the pace of your lifestyle and commitments, it may be God's way of telling you to reprioritize. But where can you possibly cut back? Here are some time stealers to consider.

THE TELEPHONE

Eleanor is a busy mother of three children. She holds a part-time job in retail sales and happens to be one of the most organized women I know. She is a natural mentor, and many people are drawn to her.

Eleanor's phone used to ring constantly with people needing advice, wanting to vent (also known as gossip), or occasionally asking for prayer. Eventually her "ministry" began to take its toll on her family.

She found herself increasingly absorbed in trying to handle other people's problems and situations. Her family frequently had to wait while she handled an urgent phone call from one of her friends. It wasn't long before her own relationship with her family began to suffer.

"Sweetheart, take this off the stove in five minutes. I have to take this call."

"Kids, I'm on the phone! Go ask your father!"

It's easy to see how too much of this would drain any family. Eleanor discovered that the answering machine, which she had loved before the kids were born, no longer served as a convenience. In fact, the machine added things to her already extensive to-do list.

Eventually Eleanor accidentally discovered a way to minimize distractions at home—without having to engage in emotionally draining confrontations with her callers. It was a blessing in disguise the day her answering machine stopped working. When it broke, she prayerfully decided not to replace it, and she quietly obtained caller ID! Now she selects the times and the people with whom she will speak, and she makes those selections without offending anyone.

Eleanor's callers are typically divided into two categories: edifying relationships (prayer partners and mentors) and ministry opportunities (people to pray for or witness to). She now deliberately spends more time interacting with people who build her up and more time praying for people who drain her. This way Eleanor takes control over the telephone and those who want her time—not the other way around.

You are in a position to consciously decide the best use of your time. If you let them, answering machines, call waiting, pagers, and cell phones can take away your choice of how you spend your time. The broken answering machine may be your ticket to more time with your family, particularly if you can't find the time to return the call for every message left on it.

If after a hard day's work you frequently find yourself talking on the phone while stirring a pot on the stove and simultaneously shushing the kids, consider this: By dividing your time this way, you are not operating at optimum efficiency. For starters, you can't give your caller your undivided attention. Furthermore, this is not meaningful interaction between you and your children. And the clincher: You run the risk of making a mess of your dinner. (Have you ever seasoned food twice because you were distracted? I certainly have.)

If you can relate a little too well to Eleanor's story of the constantly ringing phone, then you have plenty of company. Phone time is one of the most popular nonessential time expenditures. Let's face it: Women love to gab, and there's nothing wrong with talking to friends or helping others. But if you are under the impression that you are obligated to listen, offer advice, and let anyone with problems vent to you at any time, let me encourage you with this: There is a God—and He isn't you!

The fact that you are always available may be the very thing hindering someone from a deeper walk with the Lord. It is possible to be more comfortable turning to a fallible, fallen human being than to God. But as much as any person loves another, only God can truly save. Don't hinder the Holy Spirit by taking His place in others' lives.

In God's loving providence, there are professional Christian telephone ministries available to handle emotional and spiritual crises. While there is no substitute for prayer, spending time reading the Bible, or having a nice chat with a mentor, remember an ongoing crisis may be beyond your ability—or your mentor's. For more tangible help, suggest (800) New-Life (639-5433) or (888) Need-Him (633-3446). They have someone available 24 hours a day. Also, (800) A-Family (232-6459) is available 6 A.M.–6 P.M. MST.

Let these thoughts give you strength as you begin to direct your friends and your life toward the Lord:

You are not living to please others (it's futile).
You are not living to please yourself (it's selfish).
You are living to please God!

And He loves you with an everlasting love. Furthermore, He's entrusted you with children, an indescribable gift and blessing.

Because you spend time away from your child while you work, it's vital that you be mentally at home when you're physically at home. All children have a legitimate need for their mother's time and attention.

So here's a final suggestion about how to control your telephone time: Prayerfully make a distinction between people who drain you and people who build you up. Deliberately spend more time interacting with the people who build you up, and more time praying for the people who drain you.

The Television

Delta is a nurse in the high-stress neonatal intensive care unit of a busy hospital. She is also the mother of three young children. Her story reveals how she increased the amount of quality interaction time with her family by reducing the use of television.

While Delta was pregnant with her first child, she became increasingly sensitive to the violence on television. She decided to get into the habit of watching only wholesome programming.

Despite her concerns about television, though, when her first child came along, she felt relieved when the baby was old enough to pay attention to the TV set. Thanks to the "purple dinosaur," she was *almost* able to keep up with her cooking, cleaning, and bill paying. But it didn't sit right with her. She remembered how she had vowed, in her youthful pre-baby exuberance, never to use the television as an electronic baby-sitter. Delta cut back her hours at work, but still yearned for more time with her family. That's when she realized she could use the time spent watching television to interact with them.

Just as Delta began to implement the new plan, she got pregnant again and felt exhausted. Her husband started a new job and they moved. Under stress, the temptation to go back to the videos was tremendous. Everyone (including me) questioned the viability of having a no-TV family. What would she do when she really needed the kids to be still and quiet for an hour? And isn't it meaningful interaction to watch a wholesome show on television if you do it together as a family?

Delta fought the temptation to let the TV be her baby-sitter and came up with some creative ways to keep her kids occupied when she needed to get some things done. When she needs quiet, she pulls out special project toys such as clay or markers or some other kind of craft. The kids celebrate these coveted "special" toys. Every night her children "help" her make dinner. Their creative activities keep them busy, quiet, out of danger, and nearby. Delta's children create all sorts of wonderful gifts, and they are quietly absorbed in their crafts when she needs them to be. This sounds a whole lot more enriching than my own plan for quiet. "Put on a DVD" was my motto for years!

Delta is a working mother who spends almost all her off-the-clock time finding ways to integrate home activities into quality family time. Getting out of the TV habit played a vital role in her ability to develop strong family relationships.

Why Go on the Low-TV Diet?

Even busy families seem to find the time to tie up two or more hours a day watching television, sometimes without even realizing just how much family time the TV is stealing. If you are one of those families, allow me to share with you, Working Mother, several reasons to consider putting your family on a low-television diet.

The first reason is money. In the northeastern United States, cable television can be expensive, often more than $70 per month. If a family utilizes pay-per-view, this amount can quickly escalate. There is also the cost of having your family influenced by commercials to purchase greater quantities of unnecessary things. Fiscally, cable television cannot be considered economical entertainment.

Second, can "educational" or "wholesome" programs really compare with sitting down together to read a book or have a discussion? You are face to face during conversation; you exchange ideas, thoughts, and feelings. When you read a story, you can stop and start; the book will still be there. You can make eye contact with your kids and you can fully answer questions without missing anything simply because the story waits for you and goes at your pace. Television does not.

It is not easy to maintain a conversation while watching TV. Some would argue it's rude to interrupt others while they're watching a television show, and that it would be more polite to talk later. But as a busy working mother, you know all too well there is no later. If you have only a few hours between when you get home and your kids go to bed, how reasonable is it to expect anything to happen later? It doesn't make sense to let anything other than God take such a priority in our families.

It is not my intention to suggest that every working mother should eliminate the television set from her home. Watching TV is not always bad. There are benefits derived from obtaining information and entertainment from both a visual and auditory medium. The more senses involved, the more likely the message will be able to register, which can be a great tool for learning.

Prayerfully consider, however, whether or not the television has become a stumbling block in your family's life and whether you can cut back to whatever extent the Lord leads you.

If your children prefer to spend time in their rooms watching their own particular shows on their own private sets rather than spending time together as a family, think about ways to draw them out of their rooms and into the heart of the family.

Starting the Low-TV Diet

The way to gain family cooperation is astonishingly simple. To start with, convince their father by using economics. As I mentioned before, in my area, cable television costs about $70 per month, which equals $840 per year! If Dad is fiscally minded or has a frugal disposition, he may be convinced as soon as you mention a way to save nearly $1,000 every year!

If he watches a lot of TV himself and is a sports fan, then here is a tip for you. Research the price of season tickets to his favorite local sports team. If they cost less than you're paying per year for cable, voila! Suggest he see the games in person!

If you'll promise to baby-sit without complaints when he wants to go to a game, 99 percent of the sports fans in the world would support getting rid of cable and satellite TV. There is a benefit for you. No sport is played all year long, and they all have games away from home as well as weather cancellations. Consequently, during the entire off-season the whole family can enjoy life with fewer TV distractions. With prayer and God's grace, you may actually net more hours of real family time by resorting to the "season ticket" strategy.

How will you get the kids to accept cutting back or cutting out TV without significant emotional turmoil? Start by explaining and describing the benefits they will receive when they minimize the use of television for entertainment. Paint a verbal picture for them of how they will experience more of the things they already enjoy about family life.

This is important. There is an age-old adage called "WIIFM." The concept of WIIFM answers the unspoken question in everyone's heart: "What's In It For Me?" There is a difference in telling someone, "This is for your own good," versus describing all the specific good that will occur for him or her.

You won't disappoint your kids if you do your homework. For example, if your 10-year-old loves to play chess, by all means talk about what it will be like to have time to regularly play chess. If your preteen likes baking, describe the confections she will have the time to create and how her treats will amaze the family. Describe the reception she'll receive at school when she comes in with samples!

There are myriad benefits to motivate children of all ages. You can probably think of other ideas to motivate yours. Find a way to tie them in with compliance to the new family policy.

If you aren't sure what they would enjoy, then ask the question, "Other than watching TV or playing video games, what do you like to do at home the most?" When you ask the question *before* you unveil the low-television diet, their answers will provide the keys to motivating each particular child and will also give you some insight into their world.

A word to the wise: Decide in advance a reasonable amount of television time for the whole family. Dividing up time for each family member's television show and DVD preferences creates the possibility of dividing up your family's interaction time.

Consider instituting rewards for compliance, especially compliance without complaints. An extra bedtime story for the little ones, a board game with older ones, or even special "coffee break

with Mom" times for adolescents may go a long way toward motivating the family to make the adjustment. Trust your instincts.
You know what will best motivate your children.

Even if they vehemently protest initially (and some of them
will), cutting back on outside commitments, telephone time, and
television may be the right things to do for your family. And you
might even be able to think of more ways to decrease time wasters
and increase family time. Your family will become acclimated to
a simplified lifestyle, and your family dynamics will be infinitely
richer because of it.

❋ PRAYER

Lord,

*I recognize that I'm overcommitted. This burden is not
easy, nor is it light. Everything I participate in is good, but
the sum of so many good things is evidently too heavy for
me to carry.*

*I ask You to give me vision to see what I should elimi-
nate, give me the courage to let it go, then bless me with
peace and strength when I make the changes.*

*Soften the hearts of my family, friends, church, and
civic committees. Let them accept these changes with grace.
Put the desire to take charge of the good things I relinquish
into the heart of someone else.*

*I'm excited at the prospect of increasing the quality of
time I spend with my family, Lord. I praise You for blessing
me with Your love and acceptance. I'm grateful Your favor
is a gift, not dependent on my activities or my human
goodness.*

Never let me forget that when I try to earn Your blessings with my "good" activities, it becomes wages . . . and I already work enough. Remind me You've given me a free will and the promise of peace and joy.

I can't please everyone, and trying to do so has run me ragged. Help me to concentrate on pleasing You alone.

Amen.

❀ FAITH IN ACTION

List all the extraneous activities in your life.

Which of these would have to be eliminated to increase the number of meals your family can share together every week?

What steps will you have to take to simplify your family life? List them.

❋ BETWEEN FRIENDS

1. What pulls your family's at-home time apart the most—the TV, computer, or phone?

2. What ideas can you think of to motivate your children to cut back on some activities?

3. Can you think of extraneous activities at work that you can cut back on to reduce stress and bring more peace to your soul?

Start Delegating

You'll burn out, and the people right along with you.
This is way too much for you—you can't do this alone.
—Exodus 18:18

Delegate? "I don't have time to delegate!"

"I don't have anyone to delegate to!"

"They wouldn't do it right."

"I'd have to fight to get them to do it, then I'd have to inspect it once it's done. It's easier to just do it myself."

I hear you. I've been there myself. But there's a secret you've probably never been privy to. It goes beyond wishing someone else would lend a hand and complaining if he or she doesn't. It's time for action. You need real solutions to make delegation actually happen.

You have taken the first step and decided to pray with prayer partners.

And you have decided to eliminate extraneous activities. Congratulations, that's a great start. What's left in your life now cannot be eliminated and must be done.

But here's the question all moms have to consider: Does it really have to be done by *you*?

If the scripture verse at the beginning of this chapter resonates deep within you, or if it seems God is specifically talking about *your* life, then this is for you: You simply can't do it all by yourself, and God doesn't expect you to.

It's always tough to delegate, but for a busy working mom, it can seem almost impossible. To use an analogy, being a working mom is very much like juggling. Learning to juggle takes practice, and it's especially stressful if the items you juggle are valuable and fragile.

It's hard to juggle three things, harder still to juggle four. Difficulty and stress increase with each addition. Ultimately, even the best jugglers will drop a ball. This is precisely what every working mom wishes to avoid while trying to keep up with schedules, relationships, work demands, and running a household.

When you're juggling so many things, just trying to stop so you can reduce the number increases the risk of dropping something. This is the inherent risk in deciding whether and how to delegate. Believe me, I know you can't afford to let anything drop. However, you should be aware of the flip side to managing everything yourself. Sooner or later, your body will give out. Then you may be unable to do anything for weeks or months.

The tension from maintaining a high-stress lifestyle may show up as frequent headaches, muscle tightness, or a constantly churning stomach. Constant stress leads to anxiety, and in the worst-case scenario, panic attacks. Take it from me, one way or another your body and mind will not allow you to keep up more than you can bear.

Fortunately, there is hope—even for the tough case of a single working mom with young children and limited finances. The key is delegation. Every working mom can successfully delegate some of her responsibilities. If you're uncomfortable or out of practice, start out small and delegate more as you see how well things are working. There are benefits to everyone (including you) when you delegate your workload appropriately.

Find Creative Solutions

Deanna, a former work-outside-the-home mom of four, shared an innovative solution with me. When she was a working mom, the most difficult part of the day was getting dinner ready. She suspected other working moms might have the same problem. After she became a stay-at-home-mom, she called a few of her friends and asked if they would like her to make extra portions of what she planned to cook for dinner.

Deanna began putting an entire meal in disposable containers and leaving it at the doorstep of her working friends' houses in exchange for a portion of their families' grocery/takeout budgets. Since Deanna buys in bulk now, the food costs are lower, and she can pocket the extra cash. Remember, it's not extra work for Deanna because it's what she's cooking for her family anyway. Now a few working moms get to come home to an inexpensive, hot, home-cooked meal!

If any of your friends are stay-at-home moms, find out if they would be willing to give this a try one or two days a week. Just imagine coming home after a hard day's work to be greeted by the smell of an already prepared dinner. Now that's a blessing!

The Man Around the House

The question always arises concerning the household workload and what "he" ought to do versus what "she" does. I'll share with you three bits of advice I received from my mother on my wedding day:

"First, lower your expectations, Sabrina."

"Second, laugh at his jokes."

"Third, remember that a marriage requires 100 percent flexibility—and 90 percent of the flexing comes from the wife."

The last piece of advice sounded downright silly and old-fashioned to me. I thought to myself, *Maybe in your generation, Mom, but we're going to have a 50-50 marriage.*

Like most newlyweds, I found out that my expectations of marriage and the reality were two different things. My husband, Dan, later explained to me why he thinks my mom was right. Few things in marriage cause more sadness and heartbreak than unmet expectations. Generally speaking, it's more pleasant to have your expectations exceeded than to experience the disappointment of being let down. Lowering our expectations gives us a chance to be pleasantly surprised when someone exceeds them.

Next, when you laugh at someone's jokes, it is the most sincere form of applause. It opens the door to a great deal of joy. As the Bible says, "A cheerful heart is good medicine" (Proverbs 17:22, NIV).

Lastly, it's easy to recognize when you accommodate, or flex, for your spouse. It's never as clear when someone else is flexing for you. Even if a 50-50 partnership were possible in marriage, you would *always* be more aware of your effort than his. *Always.*

I suggest that you be very careful and prayerful about delegating to your husband. The temptation to go on the "must-be-nice-to-live-like-you-do" bandwagon is nearly impossible to resist. And this bandwagon is ultimately counterproductive. Believe me, I've tried it.

You probably work as hard as he does. You may even do more than the majority of women you know. But expecting him to be an assistant homemaker will almost certainly lead to disappointment.

Try to remember, most men today contribute more around the house than their own fathers did. And if you keep a running mental tally of your tasks versus his, it will not lead to a harmonious family life.

It just won't. I've tried that too.

Throw Away the Scorecard

You'll be better off if you resist the temptation to compare your workloads. The Bible calls this keeping "score of the sins of others" in 1 Corinthians 13:5. You have a choice: Is it more important to prove yourself "right" or to have peace and harmony in your home? When you need affirmation, appreciation, and understanding for all you do and you don't have a husband who'll give it to you, go to the Lord and your girlfriends!

Look at the concordance in the back of your Bible for passages about God's love for you and read them. Then go to your prayer partners and mentors for a little hands-on encouragement. It will be a lot easier to tear up your scorecard when you are filled with God's love.

Practically speaking, what's an overstressed, overburdened working mom to do? I'll tell you what I did. First, I prayed about my situation frequently. Next, I resolved to pay closer attention to Dan's strengths and look for ways he could contribute toward managing our family in a manner that would naturally suit his personality and talents. "Lord, show me how we can both use our strengths," I prayed. God was quick to show me the way.

Big Dan is a playful guy, and he loves to spend time horsing around with the kids. Whenever he gave the kids their baths, they had a great time and got clean, but the watery, soapy mess they left behind was simply something else for me to clean up (or nag about). My own style of "Wet down, soap up, rinse off!" was efficient, quick, and neat, but certainly not fun. So we compromised for efficiency *and* fun.

I happen to be one of those people who is always in a hurry, and I naturally move at a fast pace. Nowadays, after dinner I usher the kids through their routine: military-style baths, pajamas, and tooth-brushing. When they're finished, Daddy swoops in like a breath of fresh air.

My husband now puts the kids to bed at night. The kids play, read stories, recount their day, and say bedtime prayers with him. I make my exit and am free to do whatever needs to be done around the house, have some time to myself, or just retire early.

There are times when the whole bedtime ordeal takes them two full hours after I leave. But after studying my husband's strengths, I observed how long, drawn-out processes don't upset him like they do me. This is a great method to utilize our respective strengths to the benefit of our entire family.

Another area where Dan has talents to contribute to the family is grocery shopping. I noticed that he takes a lot of pride in finding bargains at the store. On the occasions when he goes shopping alone, he proudly displays the receipts showing the percentage he saved using his shopper's card, scouting out sales, or buying in bulk.

So I should just let him take over the task of grocery shopping, right? Is it really so simple? Not remotely! I came up against the hurdle most of us encounter when delegating important tasks: Sometimes we have differing definitions of how to do a task.

Let me explain. I used the typical mommy-style grocery shopping method called "Walking-down-the-aisles-and-spotting-what-we-need-as-I-go-along." I certainly couldn't expect Dan to do that. When I tried to write out a list for him, I found myself mentally exhausted trying to remember everything, and it took almost as much time to make the list as it would have to go grocery shopping!

It seemed like the pros of delegating the grocery shopping equaled the cons. This quandary led me to create a grocery list that would take the guesswork and aggravation out of the process. I call it the Working Mom™ Fast-Fax Grocery List. It's a fast, thorough, one-page list that can be e-mailed or faxed. There's a sample of the grocery list in the appendix of this book, and for your convenience, there's a free, easy-to-print blank form on our Web site, www.workingmom.com. Simply put a checkmark next to what you need, print it out, and in less than three minutes you have a foolproof list.

But suppose your husband doesn't have any grocery shopping talents. Or perhaps you're a single mom. In some areas, grocery stores are now starting to deliver, and they'll do the shopping for you! All you need to do is fill out their form, select the items you need, and the store will now shop for, bag, and deliver the groceries all the way to your kitchen at the time you choose. This option is frequently available at no extra charge, and some stores even give a $10 credit off your first home delivery!

There's no downside to having your groceries delivered because any item you don't think is fresh enough or doesn't meet your approval can typically be returned for a full refund. A working mom simply cannot lose if there's a grocery store in your area that delivers. Try it; you'll like it.

A Final Word About Husbands

Every couple's needs and inclinations are different, but again, it's better to look for each partner's natural talents and preferences and make some compromises. Maybe your husband loves to grill. Ask him if he'll cook dinner on a specific night (or two) a week. Maybe he wouldn't mind folding the laundry while he watches the news. The point is to creatively and prayerfully think through the delegation question. Remember, nagging will not induce your husband to help out more, but it is guaranteed to add stress to your home life.

KIDS: THE GREAT GUILT INDUCERS

Some working moms feel that because they are away from their kids so many hours during the day, they don't want their precious time together to be spent fighting about chores. Consequently, very little is expected of the children with respect to pitching in around the house.

Anna, one of my mentors, set me straight about kids and chores with the following advice: "You've got to remember you're raising future adults, and childhood is when they learn responsibility. When you have 'your reasons' for not setting and enforcing realistic expectations, the kids will grow up to be poorly equipped to meet their own families' expectations in the future. It would be a disservice to their future spouses and children."

Put simply, all kids (even the kids of working moms) should be required to do unpaid work around the house regularly. It's for their good, and it's for *your* good!

At the risk of stating the obvious, once they're able to walk and talk, every child can pitch in. Even a two-year-old can be taught to put away toys. Three- and four-year-olds can be taught to fold washcloths and dish-towels. Once they have learned their colors, they can easily sort laundry into dark colors, light colors, and whites.

As kids get older, they have the ability to handle more work around the house. The first step in assigning household tasks is to know what they are capable of. If you are unsure what chores your kids can reasonably handle, the Working Mom™

Household Job Chart delineates typical household chores children can do at various ages. You'll find it in the appendix of this book and a free, easy-to-print version is available on www.workingmom.com.

This leads to the recurring question: "How on earth will I get them to do it?" There are multiple answers to this dilemma. To a great extent, your success will depend upon the relationship you have with your children, their personalities, and your personality. Let me make a suggestion: Remember to answer the WIIFM question. (What's In It For Me?)

Back when my brother and I were young children, the WIIFM was usually that we could avoid a spanking, lecture, and/or being grounded if we complied. For my brother, that was usually enough motivation to elicit his compliance. For me, those methods induced a sense of trepidation as I consciously chose to disobey despite the warning.

There are no quick and easy, one-size-fits-all formulas for getting every child to do what he's told. However, a consequence coupled with an incentive substantially increases the likelihood of compliance in almost every managerial situation, including motherhood.

Going back to my own situation, when I was growing up, my parents discovered they could gain remarkable compliance from their headstrong daughter when they used car privileges as an incentive. "Sabrina, I'll let you take my car out to get some ice cream if you can finish cleaning up before dark." This really motivated me.

But my parents used more than just incentives. One of their often used consequences hit me where it hurt me the most: "If this room is not cleaned up by the time I get home from work, I'm unplugging your telephone, and you won't get it back until I'm ready for you to have it!" For a very social child, this served as the hammer of punishments, the one I sought to avoid with all of my being.

However, those same tactics were completely ineffective when used on my brother. His personality is different from mine, and he fairly shrugged at either gaining car privileges or losing his telephone. But he couldn't do without his video games; thus, the loss of those served as the hammer of all consequences for him. He could be motivated by the promise of getting new basketball cards. Each child is different. Study your children carefully and it will become clear how to best motivate, as well as how to administer the most effective consequences.

What If They Get Mad at Me for This?

Some mothers describe their still-at-home children as their best friends. On the surface, this sounds idyllic, but these mothers are at a serious disadvantage in disciplinary situations. Every time discipline or correction is called for, such a mom runs the risk of losing her best friend. This creates a situation no child is mature enough to handle. For a best friend, look to your prayer partners and mentors. This is just one more reason why establishing prayer partners is the first secret to phenomenal success. You will find a frequent need for them.

Getting Things Done with Teens

What about when the kids get older? What if you have teenagers or preteens right now, and can't imagine battling over chores when it's so hard just keeping the peace?

Kimberly Chastain, Licensed Marriage and Family Therapist, is the author of *Help! My Pre-Teen/Teenager Is Driving Me Nuts* (an e-book available at www.christianworkingmom.com). Kimberly shares the following 15 survival tips for parenting preteens and teens:

1. Your children are on an emotional roller coaster due to hormonal changes and mood swings. YOU DO NOT have to ride the roller coaster with them. Don't allow your child's mood to affect yours. Acknowledge their emotions, but avoid taking on their mood.

2. Develop a thick skin. Adolescents often say mean and hateful things. Although it's unacceptable, it does happen. When kids are preparing to break away, it can be quite messy as they try to push their parents away with words. It still hurts, but don't take it to heart.

3. Set clear limits. It's tempting to give in rather than stand firm. (Adolescents are great at arguing.) But this age group still needs boundaries and limits. No one else is going to meet that need but you.

4. Do not engage in a long discussion after you have already given your decision. All teenagers are attorneys-in-training and will argue a point to its death. They hope if they bug you long enough you will give in. Inform them it's the end of the discussion and walk away.

5. When you find yourself raising your voice, take a time-out. Someone has to be the adult . . . YOU! All too often, parents end up acting like teenagers themselves. Even if they push your buttons, remember, someone has to remain calm. Instead, try lowering your voice whenever your teenager raises his or hers.

6. Have your own support group. When kids are little, parents share everything with their friends. Once they become teenagers, parents don't share as much. Talk to other parents and find out what "everyone else" is doing. Decide to establish a group curfew, keeping everyone on the same page. There is strength in numbers. (Just look at the teenagers!)

7. Enlist other adults who share your values to talk to your children. As hard as it is to admit, often teenagers will talk to anyone except their parents. Sometimes it helps to have another adult to confide in whose advice you trust.

8. Take each and every opportunity to listen when they want to talk. This may not happen very often, so it's important that you drop everything to listen. It may happen late at night. If your child finally decides to open up with you, then you need to be all ears. Remember, God gave you two ears and one mouth. That means you should be listening twice as much as you speak.

9. Choose your battles. Are you on your child's case every day about something? At some point, let it go. Don't be a permanent nag. The big battles are: drugs, alcohol, and sex. Since kids listen to a limited amount of what parents have to say, better that they hear the important messages, not just that their rooms are a mess. When tempted to nag, ask yourself "Will this matter 10 years from now?"

10. Use captive moments in the car to talk. It seems teenagers do their best talking when they don't have to make eye contact. And in the car they can't run away. Some of your best conversations can take place while driving to the next activity.

11. Get to know their friends and be willing to allow them to come to your home. You'll know what's going on better than if they were at someone else's house. Often, your teen's friends will tell you things about your child you didn't know. It helps to keep you informed.

12. Find the actions and behaviors your child is doing well and tell him. Look for opportunities to praise your child. Call attention to his admirable personality characteristics. Even a headstrong, stubborn child has a positive aspect. Determination, persistence, and a stick-to-it mentality will benefit him later in life. His ability to persevere is admirable.

13. Be prepared to admit when you're wrong and ask your children for forgiveness. After all, it's what you expect from them. You will gain a great deal of respect from your teenager by admitting when you are wrong. All too often, teenagers tell me their parents have never asked them for forgiveness because the parents have not once admitted they were wrong.

14. Teenagers want to spend time with their parents, but will rarely admit it or ask to do it. Make sure they are on your to-do list, especially when things have been difficult. They need reminders that they are a priority in your life.

15. Remember the famous saying, "This too shall pass." Sometimes a parent needs to just hang on until they get through a difficult time. It will get better. I know there are times when it doesn't seem possible. But this too shall pass. Remember when your children were babies and it seemed they would never get out of diapers?

PROFESSIONAL HELP

Even with the entire family pitching in around the house, if finances allow, bringing in an occasional cleaning service or a periodic housekeeper can free up a lot of time and energy. The housekeeper can do the heavy or complicated jobs kids aren't able to do and you don't have time to do. I highly recommend it. Ask your acquaintances if they know of a housekeeper who's trustworthy and thorough. If you have to resort to the phone book or an advertisement in your neighborhood, be sure to check the references.

I have a friend who lived far from family when she had her first child. She returned to work full-time but refused to hire a housekeeper even though there was enough money in the family budget. She said that every time she brought someone in, that person didn't do as good a job as she could do herself. She figured, why pay someone to do a worse job than she could do?

She tried to keep her demanding job, an immaculate house, and nurture a new baby and her relationship with her husband, but it was simply exhausting. Everything began to unravel within a few months.

She and her husband ended up quitting their jobs and moving closer to family. They are both doing well now, but when I think of all the needless stress they went through because she was unwilling to accept "mediocre" help, it makes me consider how different things could have been.

DELEGATING ON THE JOB

Although situations vary with each job, there's almost always something crying out to be delegated to someone else. School teachers sometimes give extra credit to students who volunteer to help clean up the classroom or do other chores. This is a wonderful way to delegate and get home more quickly.

But certain work situations don't easily lend themselves to delegation. For example, take the case of the secretary who regularly washes the office dishes and buys the half-and-half—without compensation. Depending on the corporate culture, she may be able to negotiate a little extra time off and/or pay for herself if she can't get out of doing these things. How? By keeping a running log of exactly how much time she spends performing ancillary duties! If the time is substantial, any employer might decide it's better for the company's bottom line to provide paper cups, utensils, and creamer. Or a supervisor may post a sign to remind everyone: "Your mother doesn't work here. If you use it, wash it, dry it, and put it away!—The Management " (Yes, I've actually seen this note posted in an office kitchen.)

A more subtle but equally effective idea is for the company to order a personalized coffee mug for each person in the office and ask everyone to keep his or her mug clean. Thereafter, it'll be obvious who left his or her mug in the sink.

Finding Solutions

In a career situation where the workload is unbearable, it's necessary to find out *exactly* what is eating up so much on-the-clock time. Once you determine this, you can look for a solution or alternative to resolve it to the benefit of the company and/or your supervisor.

As soon as you approach your supervisor, it's imperative that you answer the WIIFM question. This is the question running through your supervisor's mind the entire time you're speaking. For your own sake, make sure *how the company will benefit* is the first thing out of your mouth. When you start a request for change by answering the WIIFM question, you are much more likely to get what you want. People make changes because there's something in it for *them*.

My son mastered this concept by the time he was five years old. Whenever he wants something, he will approach people with the benefits *they* will receive. Here's a sample conversation from his younger days:

> "Mommy, if you let me have a piece of candy, I promise I'll eat all my dinner. One piece of candy for me right now will give you a nice, happy dinner."
>
> "I don't know, sweetheart. You've got to practice writing your name, and I'm concerned the sugar will make it hard for you to sit still and concentrate."

"No it won't, Mom. I'll be so happy you gave me my candy that I'll go straight to the table and do my work. You won't have a hard time about homework—if you let me eat my candy."

Under the cross-examination from the master litigator, I begin to waffle. After all, a willingness to do homework and a happy dinner are hard to resist.

"Are you sure you won't spoil your appetite and you'll do your homework—with no hard time?"

"Positive, Mommy," he says, already sensing victory.

"Okay, Daniel. One piece. Please don't make me regret this."

"I won't, Mom. You're the best mother in the whole world!" he says emphatically, smoothing over my lingering doubts with lavish praise.

Notice how he never once talked about how badly *he* wanted or needed the candy? Could I see he was really motivated by his own benefit? Of course I could. Was I motivated to comply with his request anyway? You'd better believe it!

If you think your current workload should be split between two people, or you want to change your hours, condense your workweek, or even work from home, think long and hard about what's in it for *everyone else* if your request is granted. Write it down. Refine it. Show it to your mentors. Then request a meeting with your supervisor to present an idea you've been working on to increase productivity.

I can't emphasize this enough: *Don't go to your supervisor unless your solution has a strong benefit for the company, preferably with direct benefits to the person deciding whether or not to grant your request!* Presenting a problem with no workable solution in the company's best interest is called a complaint, and managers/

supervisors often don't respond well to complaints (or complainers). A complaint from a person reputed to be a complainer will seldom change anything. Bottom line: You won't get what you want by complaining.

THE SUPERWOMAN MYTH

Before we leave this topic, I want to go back to the main reason many women don't delegate enough: impossibly high standards. You may be able to do a particular task better than anyone else in your company. You may be able to manage the house better than your husband ever could. You can probably fold laundry straighter than the kids, and you likely can clean your house the way you like it better than any housekeeper. But Superwoman does not exist. When you try to impersonate her, you aren't fooling anyone. Don't shoot yourself in the foot by expecting everyone to do things to some impossibly high standard. Accept the help you can get, and be grateful for it. Once you learn to relax a little bit, you'll be glad you did.

❀ PRAYER

Lord,

There's so much to be done, and so few people to help me do it. Help the rest of the family see our needs and respond. I don't want to be an exacting taskmaster.

Help me to delegate some of my responsibilities in a loving manner. Make those whom I ask receive these tasks with an open heart and a willing spirit. Give me the courage to risk being temporarily unpopular with the kids as I introduce and enforce these requirements.

Losing control over the details of maintaining our home is frightening to me. Help me not to overreact or give up when things don't meet my expectations.

You are in control, Lord. Enable me to rest safely in the knowledge that You are always with us, and You love my family more than I possibly could. Lord, I believe. Help me with my doubts.

Amen.

❀ FAITH IN ACTION

In what ways might perfectionism be keeping you from delegating tasks to your children? How about guilt?

List the top three things you could delegate to members of your family. Will you need to train them? Set a date and time to show them how to do each task.

Are there things at work you could delegate, thereby reducing your stress level? List them along with the people you might delegate to.

Think about your attitude toward your husband. Is there resentment because you feel your workloads are uneven? Set aside a time to ask him what tasks he thinks he's good at or enjoys doing.

❈ BETWEEN FRIENDS

1. What holds you back from delegating the things you probably shouldn't be doing?

2. Ask each other for a few ideas on how you can overcome the things stopping you.

Learn to Multitask

*She sets about her work vigorously; her arms are strong
for her tasks. She sees that her trading is profitable,
and her lamp does not go out at night.*
—Proverbs 31:17-18, NIV

There is only one place in the entire Bible where you'll find the plural form of the word *task*. This verse refers to a woman who has:
- a husband,
- children,
- a job in real estate,
- another job selling garments,
- servants to manage,
- and a busy household to run.

She's a working mother! Even though Proverbs 31 mentions that this working mother has servants, God knows that with so much on her plate, she still has multiple tasks to accomplish.

In His infinite wisdom, God has left us the "Basic Instructions Before Leaving Earth" manual (an acrostic for BIBLE), giving us markers of the way in which we should go. In our times, we call this ability to accomplish more than one thing at the same time "multitasking."

Successful implementation of this skill will make you more productive, free up time, and reduce stress. Overall, it will be more enjoyable to get through a busy day.

Perhaps this is an appropriate place to point out why I included stories of other working moms in this book. It's because my own wisdom and knowledge would barely fill up a pamphlet, let alone a book. Such was the case with multitasking. I admit that I had to be convinced when I was first introduced to the concept. I thought it would stress me out and make me more likely to drop the ball on something. Now I can't imagine life without it.

LESSONS FROM A MASTER MULTITASKER

Celine is a woman who is naturally very efficient. She's organized, dependable, and punctual. Almost nothing rattles her. Do you recall the typical morning scenario at the beginning of this book? The one with no meat taken out of the freezer for dinner, a sink full of dishes, and the husband down to his last pair of clean underwear?

Well, I proposed the following challenge to my friend Celine: "What would you do when you came home on a night like this?"

After thinking for a moment she responded: "I would sit the kids down at the table and give them a light snack. Then I would go downstairs and put a load of laundry in the washing machine."

At this point I interrupted her with the following excuse: "Oh, Celine, my kids wouldn't eat dinner if I gave them a snack so close to dinner time. And I can always do laundry after they're asleep."

Undaunted, Celine continued with the following counsel: "Sabrina, never forget that in front of the washing machine is an excellent place to cry and pray. And if you give the kids something light to snack on, they won't be starving, irritable, and breathing down your neck while you're making dinner. While you're putting clothes in the washing machine, you can pray and think about what to do next. Then no matter what you decide to do, you'll at least be doing something about the dirty clothes. You can wash clothes, start the dishwasher, cook dinner, and get the kids started on homework all at the same time!"

The expression "I can do only one thing at a time" simply does not apply to mothers who work both inside and outside of the home. In order to be effective, occasionally you are going to have to do two or three things at once. Ever since your first child was a minute old, you have had to multitask. Think about the standard labor-and-delivery scenario of feeding the baby while you smile for the camera and answer the doctor's questions!

Freeing Up Time Equals Freeing Up Space

Let's use a child's set of stackable wooden blocks to illustrate. Toddlers go through a stage where they line the blocks all up end to end, creating a long straight train. This is wonderful, except it takes up room, so it's natural to insist they stack them up somewhere when they're done playing. (This conserves floor space.) The blocks can't be stacked too high or they will fall. They need to be stacked low enough not to fall over, but high enough to open up floor space. A balanced ratio between the two is needed.

Try to think of multitasking as stacking your activities one on top of another so you can free up your time. In Celine's scenario, by giving the kids a snack, starting laundry, praying, then tackling the dishes and dinner, she stacked five tasks into a one-hour time period. And we can all learn to think and prioritize like this—especially in the midst of less-than-ideal circumstances.

What's in It for You?
1. Increased productivity.
2. More free time.
3. Energy savings.

From the time you wake up in the morning until you go back to bed at night, try to think of things in your usual routine to multitask. Don't forget that you can even do some things while you're still asleep! For example, you could put the ingredients in the bread maker the night before and wake up to fresh bread or a coffee cake for breakfast. That makes breakfast a snap.

You can use a coffeemaker with a built-in timer. Set it for the time you need to wake up, then set it to keep the burner on for a half an hour. The smell of the coffee is an incentive to wake up. Not to mention that you'd better get it while it's fresh-brewed and still hot. For some people, this is a powerful incentive to get out of bed.

Even if you forget to set it up the night before, you could still multitask coffee making with shower-taking—two tasks at once. While waiting for the water to warm up, you could brush your teeth—three tasks at once. You could even shave with Nair hair remover—that's four tasks at the same time. Multitasking in the morning will help you get up and out of the house with less hassle.

Once multitasking becomes natural to you, you'll think of even more ways to save time and energy, which translates into more free time for your family. The idea is to make a game out of finding ways to multitask. Let's look at a time waster that can become a time saver.

The Commute

Getting back and forth to work each day represents a significant block of time for some people. Most people try to use the time in their car, train, or bus to unwind. After all, there doesn't seem to be much else to do while fighting traffic.

Actually, there are ways to unwind, stimulate the imagination, teach, and learn eternal truths all while being entertained and getting to work. Here are a few suggestions:

- Catch up on all the books you've been meaning to read but haven't found time for. More and more audio books are being recorded on cassette or CD, so even if you're driving you can "read."
- Listen to inspirational music. I find classical and contemporary Christian to be the most uplifting, but listen to whatever inspires and either energizes you or helps you relax and de-stress.
- Listen to the Bible on CD, cassette, or MP3. It's simply the best way to refresh your soul.
- Listen to Focus on the Family Radio Theatre on CD. It's the best tip I know for traveling with kids in the car. The programs are available in bookstores and on the Web site, www.family.org. I've seen firsthand how the Radio Theatre dramatization of *The Chronicles of Narnia* by C.S. Lewis dramatically improves the dynamics of driving with kids in the car. There is simply no better way to introduce children to great literature, stimulate their imaginations, reinforce family values, and transform the kid-commute into something everyone looks forward to. Commuting can be as smooth as silk. Even with a teenager!

Here are a few ways to save time at work or home by using the time in the train, bus, or carpool to get a few tasks done:

- If you ride the bus or train, read the newspaper or professional journals while riding so you don't take that time away from your job or family.
- Take along some mending or needlework, if you're so inclined.

- Use the time to go over your schedule, make lists, or pre-pare presentations.
- Write and address your Christmas cards.

Multitasking on the Job

I purposely am not going to address multitasking on the job because of the huge differences in job descriptions. However, once you start multitasking at home and on your commute, you'll naturally start looking for ways to stack your tasks on the job too. Begin by observing your colleagues, or by asking a mentor how she accomplishes more in her day. Examine your own job for time wasters that lend themselves to multitasking. Again, make a game out of finding ways to save time and energy on the job, and soon you'll be accomplishing more in less time.

First Things First—with Good Reason!

A word of warning: I strongly urge you to begin perfecting your multitasking skills *after* you have implemented the previous three secrets into your usual routine. First, ask for God's guidance in prayer, then pare down your commitments and unproductive time wasters. Next, delegate appropriately.

After you have implemented the first three secrets, you are ready to perfect the art of multitasking to make the most of your time, energy, and relationships. However, if you start multitask-ing before the other areas of your life are in order, you won't increase your productivity at all! It would be like taking the expressway to burnout instead of the scenic route.

It is an eye-opener to think about how much more you can accomplish by implementing the first four secrets. The big bonus to multitasking is the increased free time to do what's really important to you. It's another answer to prayer.

❄ PRAYER

Lord,

You are a marvelous, gracious, loving God. I'm so grateful You take an interest in even the smallest details of my life. I want to do only what You consider to be the best for my family and me. I ask You to bless me with amazing direction and productivity. Give me the energy to accomplish things in harmony with Your will.

Bless me with a cheerful attitude. Keep me ever mindful that showing my love for my family and spending time with my family come before checking off activities on my to-do list.

Somehow, Lord, make me productive, loving, patient, and joyful—all at the same time. You are the God of all possibilities, and I ask for this miracle with the trusting faith of a child.

Amen.

❀ FAITH IN ACTION

List three things you can multitask regularly in the morning and three you can multitask in the evening.

What can you do to make your commute more productive?

List three ways you can be more productive at work by stacking tasks.

✻ Between Friends

1. Have you ever tried to multitask too many things at once? What happened?

2. What would you do differently in life if you had it to do all over again?

Show Up Big Time

*Dear friend, take my advice; it will add years
to your life. I'm writing out clear directions
to Wisdom Way, I'm drawing a map to Righteous
Road. I don't want you ending up in blind
alleys, or wasting time making wrong turns.*
—PROVERBS 4:10-11

Consider Secret 5 to be the unwritten rule of the workplace. It's likely no one you trust has ever pulled you aside to clue you in on exactly how to be a great employee *and* a great mom. The majority of working moms learn the unwritten rules of succeeding in the workplace and at home the hard way—by making a lot of mistakes.

Childless women in the workplace don't usually know these secret rules exist, and these unwritten rules don't always apply to working dads. Experienced working moms know the rules but may be unsure if they can trust you enough to give you this warning. Right now, think of me as an experienced working mom pulling you aside to give you some insider's workplace advice.

Start by being aware of the still widely held stereotypes and prejudices against mothers in the workplace. These are just a few of the perceptions you may find yourself up against because you are a working mom:

- She won't be able to handle the job.
- Her performance is slipping.
- You can't depend on her.
- She'll quit the first chance she gets.
- She doesn't want to be here.
- She'll do the minimum required to keep her job.
- Her family makes more work for everybody else.

In all honesty, the same things could be said about *any* employee, regardless of his or her family situation. But if you're a working mother who is absent from work, late getting there, or has to leave early to take care of the kids, watch out! Even if everybody else comes in late, calls in sick, and goofs off, *it will stand out more when you do it.* Being a working mom who is guilty of taking the same liberties as everyone else is just like putting a target on your back. While it's possible that no one will take aim at you, it sure makes you an easy mark.

That isn't fair.

That isn't right.

It might not even be legal.

Somebody ought to do something!

True, somebody really ought to buck the system and change things. Someone truly does need to shake things up in the modern workplace. If you feel called to be the person, I (along with countless others) will be grateful to you.

But if directly fighting against these stereotypes and prejudices seems like more than you wish to tackle at this point in your life (and most working moms don't have time to take on the corporate culture), here's the secret to helping you avoid them—and maybe even eliminate them in some small measure. The secret is to *be a consummate professional,* no matter what your job title is.

How to Be a Consummate Professional

As you can imagine, coming in late and missing work for one reason or another will make a small minority of people resent you. This is especially true if it creates hardship for others and they feel you're not carrying your share of the workload. This can make trouble for you when it begins to escalate to verbal jabs, potshots taken at you behind your back, or putdowns cloaked in the guise of teasing humor that can occur right to your face.

It usually begins with lighthearted remarks about your dependability, commitment, and contribution in the workplace, and seemingly good-natured references to how you probably *won't* be able to do something because of your kids.

These do not always spell impending disaster, but they should be considered red flags. Once you are in the position of needing to prove yourself, it will consume time and energy better spent doing your job and being with your family. Remember, in the working world, it's always easier to maintain a good reputation than to rebuild one.

That's Already Happening—What Now?

Don't worry, here's the plan if you've suddenly realized you have a minor public relations drama unfolding. It's pretty easy to turn your reputation around, and with it, find yourself experiencing the flexibility to be able to respond to occasional child-related issues.

The first thing you need to do is to show up. I can't emphasize enough how much better your quality of life at home and at work will be if you show up a little bit early for work every day. *Yes, I said early.*

Being early is exponentially better than on time. And it leaves "just a few minutes late" in the dust as far as perception goes, not to mention how it improves your quality of life. Think about it this

way: If you have your coat off and are busily at work when everyone else starts trickling in, it's nearly impossible for anyone to ever
question your dependability. You'll beat the traffic, get a close park-
ing spot at work, and you'll get an incredible amount of work done
on projects before the typical workday interruptions start. Getting
to work 10 to15 minutes early will significantly reduce your overall stress level and make you more productive—not to mention increasing your standing in the eyes of your supervisor and coworkers.

However, you should not do this at the expense of your family. If getting to work earlier means rushing your children and
spending significantly less time with them each day, then it may
not be right for you. If, on the other hand, you are organized and
ready to go when your kids get on the bus or need to be dropped
off, then getting to work a little earlier can make your whole day
run more smoothly and calmly.

Your First Priority

The greatest challenge to showing up big time is establishing safe,
reliable, and enriching care for your children while you're at work.
Depending on the age of your children, this could be a baby-sitter,
preschool, grade school, an after-school program, or a latchkey for
teens. Setting up a Plan A, Plan B, Plan C, and Plan D for childcare will significantly maximize your dependability as an employee.

Plan A is your usual working/childcare routine. Plan B is the
routine you follow when your child is sick, or school is closed but
work is not. Plan C is for when Plan B falls through. Plan D is
the plan of last resort.

Plan A
Most likely, you already have a Plan A scenario to care for your
child while you work. For babies and toddlers, this would be their

baby-sitter or daycare. For school-age kids, this is a regular school day and before- or after-school programs. For teenagers, this might include a latchkey. If your usual routine could use some tweaking, the following tips will make it easier to set up a better functioning one for your family.

Start with something that will work *right now*. Don't spend a lot of time worrying about what might be needed in another year or two. Meet your current needs as best as you can. Why compromise on childcare that works for now in anticipation of what might be needed later?

In the case of babies and toddlers, the more individualized, quality care you can provide, the better. This can include having a trusted relative baby-sit, hiring a nanny or au pair, or even working opposite shifts from your spouse so that one of you is always with your child.

The positives of having one-on-one care for your child are:

- Your child will have a caregiver's undivided attention.
- Your child will be frequently held, attended to, and nurtured.
- If the childcare is in your own home, this is another positive. Your mornings and evenings will run a whole lot more smoothly when you don't have to pack up your child, lunches, and a diaper bag.

At young ages, you needn't be overly concerned about curriculum; the primary lesson young children need to learn is that they are safe, secure, and loved.

The negatives of having one-on-one childcare are:

- If your caregiver is sick or unable to care for your child, you'll need a ready replacement.
- Having a one-on-one childcare provider can also be expensive. And a live-in nanny or au pair can intrude on your family life.

• You also are placing a great deal of trust in this individual. It is vitally important that you check the background of anyone who will be left alone with your child.

There are now widely available means of finding out about the person you are considering to care for your child. Look on www.workingmom.com for information about how to obtain an inexpensive background check. The peace of mind you get from having as much information as possible about a childcare provider is invaluable.

Nanny-cams have become popular in recent years. These are small surveillance cameras that can be put up throughout your home. If you are going to have one installed in your home, it's wise to inform potential applicants from the start. As the saying goes, an ounce of prevention is worth a pound of cure. Your child's safety is more important than the risk of offending an applicant. It's also nice to know in advance if your childcare provider would object to your scrutiny.

Rather than one-on-one in-home care, some families opt to utilize a family daycare. This is a person who takes care of several children in her home during the day. The positives are:
• This is a home-like setting.
• There may be only a few other children in the home.
• The caregiver is very likely to have experience with children; she may be a mom or grandmother herself.
• It is generally less expensive than a nanny or au pair.
The negatives are:
• If the caregiver is sick or unavailable, there may not be a ready replacement.
• Some family daycare providers are not as rigidly regulated as professional daycare centers. Furthermore, installing a nanny-cam is usually out of the question—after all, it's not your house.

Professional preschools are one of the most widely utilized childcare options.

The positives of preschools are:

- Early and late drop off.
- More options if the regular caregiver or teacher is sick.
- Typically they have an educational curriculum in place.
- They are regulated to some extent by state or local government.

The negatives of preschool are:

- High turnover in staff.
- A higher incidence of sickness among kids.
- Your child has to share the attention of the caregiver.

It is possible to utilize a combination of these childcare resources. In fact, combining options is the ticket to being able to show up big time at work. I'll give you an example of how our family does it.

In our family, we have a trusted relative come to our home to care for each baby until he or she is old enough to attend preschool. However, there is a back-up plan in case the caregiver is sick, on vacation, or otherwise unavailable. This is called Plan B, and it is essential to reduce the number of days my husband and I miss work.

Plan B

Your Plan B for childcare is utilized when a child is sick, or if schools are closed but work is not. This scenario is the most likely to affect work performance and employee attendance. However, it doesn't have to cause major upheaval if you plan for the unexpected in advance. In our case, I asked my prayer partners, mentors, and trusted friends who are stay-at-home moms if they would mind being one of several people I could call on if I found myself in a last-minute scramble for childcare. I described the most likely scenario to be an unexpected school closing or a mildly ill child. Generally speaking, people are more willing to lend a helping hand if it's a one-time event versus a long-term commitment.

There's another advantage when you have a preset course of action in place. If you have spoken with people before the need arises, you won't have to feel as if you are calling "out of the blue" to ask for a favor. It's much easier to ask for help if you have pre-qualified the potential request.

For younger children, many preschools will allow you to register your child to attend on a "per diem" (by the day, if space allows) basis. Even if your child normally has one-on-one care, you will be grateful you took the time to proactively preregister when Plan A childcare falls through.

Start by checking with the newer preschools in your area. When they first open their doors, many schools are still building their enrollment and are more likely to allow preregistered children on an as-needed basis. Usually, all you have to do is fill out the application, pay the registration fee and the cost of the day's care, and keep your child's immunization records up to date.

"Expect the unexpected." Consider this to be the mantra of life as a working mother. Establish a plan to address the inevitable turn of events that will leave you in the lurch for childcare. This is not an "if" question, it is a "when" question.

What separates the women from the girls is whether there is a proactive plan to respond—other than staying home from work. The primary benefit to having Plan B in place is putting an end to the desperate mad dash that occurs when a child can't go to school.

Plan C

Sometimes only you will do. If your child is more than mildly ill, or if your Plan B falls through, either you or your spouse will have to take time off work to care for your child. The way to go about it varies depending on your company's written (and unwritten) policy on sick-child time.

Let me encourage you to do the following: Minimize your own use of sick days for yourself whenever humanly possible. This serves a two-fold purpose. If you have a reputation for rarely missing a day's work, it serves you well during the times when you absolutely need to be gone. But remember, no one at work wants your germs any more than you want theirs. And don't halfway kill yourself by working when you need to take the time to heal. You'll only make things worse. So reserve sick days for when you are sick with communicable diseases or when your child needs you.

You will have to prayerfully consider how much information you give when you call in sick to care for a child. As a general rule, less is more. Women tend to offer more explanations for their actions than men. If you always feel tongue-tied when you call in, here are some standard answers you can personalize to suit your style:

"I won't be coming in today."

"I'm going to take a sick day today."

"I'll need to use a personal day today."

Did you notice all three examples are statements? No questions. No *asking* permission to be sick. You're a grown woman, not a kid in the principal's office. By all means, resist the urge to ramble.

Speak to your supervisor, not one of your coworkers or your boss's secretary. If you have to leave a message, try to do it on a voice mail, rather than having someone else write it down.

Plan D

Plan D is the plan of last resort. This is when you've gone through everyone on your Plan B list, you simply cannot call in sick (Plan C), and your child can't go to school.

You might consider bringing the child to work with you. If you do, please bring something to play with that has the potential to hold a great deal of attention. I'm not usually an advocate of pocket-sized electronic games, but this would be a good time for one.

Some local hospitals have "sick child" programs available. Call your area hospitals *in advance* to see if they have something available, then preregister, even if you seriously doubt you'll ever use it.

Lastly, you might want to allow an older child to stay home alone. This is an individual call on your part. At a minimum, your child should be responsible enough to adhere to some basic safety rules:

- No using the stove.
- No visitors.
- Answer the phone only if it's Mom or Dad.
- No Internet.
- No going outside.
- Know what you should do in an emergency.
- Know what *is* an emergency.

As a rule of thumb, my own mother did not allow my brother and me to stay at home alone until we were pretty old—nearly in high school—and I'll confess, the first time was a little scary.

Plan D should really be the plan of last resort. When all is said and done, just remember, putting a plan in place—especially a plan that includes a response to occasional catastrophes—will dispel most of the anguish involved with scrambling for quality childcare.

MAKE A BIG-TIME IMPRESSION

Now you are ready to show up for work, so it's time to learn how to do it "big time." The Bible emphasizes the importance of humility, but it also warns against false humility: "Let no one cheat you of your reward, taking delight in false humility" (Colossians 2:18, NKJV).

If you have done a good job, you might think it should speak for itself. Maybe it will, but maybe it won't. And if you work in the midst of a situation where someone is just waiting to pounce on one false move of yours, it would be foolhardy and naïve to think performance alone will maintain your stellar reputation. This is yet another lesson I learned in the school of hard knocks: You simply must not fall into the trap of false humility—particularly if you are a working mother.

Every workplace has employees who are regarded as "star performers." Make an assessment of the activities and characteristics most often praised about people on your job, then look at your performance in light of those characteristics. Following your job description is a good start, but it's frequently not the only criteria used to assess your performance.

In some jobs, a nebulous standard is used, such as the number of voice mails sent out, or whether you send out e-mail with the time recorded as late in the evening or early in the morning. Believe me, in some places, these things really get noticed!

Something as simple as walking at a fast pace can enhance the impression of superproductivity. Some employers gauge an employee by sales numbers, acquired new clients, or the number and speed of project completions. It can even be how many classes an employee teaches. Performance assessments will vary widely, even within the same industry. This is why it is vital that you pay attention when a colleague receives praise or recognition from others. When you listen carefully to what's said about the star performers, it serves as a guide to what you can do to make a big-time impression of your own in your particular work environment.

It's Working! What Now?

Learn to accept a compliment graciously. Practice this. I'm serious. Begin listening to how you respond to an accolade. Do you find yourself uttering falsely humble statements?

"Oh, it was nothing."

"Stop, you're embarrassing me."

"Whatever!"

This takes your big-time success and shrinks it down in an instant. It serves absolutely no purpose. Stop doing it. Discomfort with praise and recognition typically drives a woman to minimize her "moment."

Let me strengthen your resolve to accept compliments graciously by sharing God's position on the subject: "Don't call attention to yourself; let others do that for you" (Proverbs 27:2).

Please notice the word *let*. It means "allow," "permit," and "do not prohibit." Therefore, for your own sake, and by mandate of God, eradicate the negative, downplaying tendency to respond without grace to a compliment. For example, when you hear, "Great job!" or "Nice work!" respond with an affirming and direct statement:

"Thank you, I'm glad you noticed."

"That's nice to hear. Thank you for telling me."

A third party's praise holds a great deal of credibility, and is generally viewed as impartial. Think about it—isn't it hard to believe the tales of a braggart when she goes on and on about the feats she has accomplished? People seldom compliment those who have a reputation for "tooting their own horn." Maybe it's because everyone has already heard it blown so many times! You won't be a braggart if you do what Jesus commanded: "Let your light shine before men, that they may see your good deeds and praise your Father in heaven" (Matthew 5:16, NIV).

❋ PRAYER

Lord,

Let me shine for Your glory, not my own. Use me to spread Your love, mercy, and grace, even while I'm at work.

You've given me such a tremendous love for my child. I'm certain no one on earth loves this child like I do. It's so very hard to trust any person or school system to take care of this precious gift while I'm working.

I ask You, Lord of heaven and earth, to personally watch over, guard, comfort, and reassure us while we're apart.

Put a hedge of protection around my child so no harm in body, mind, or spirit will ever befall him. Enable me to make wise decisions in finding quality childcare and in keeping up with the never-ending demands upon me at work.

I know I can't do this without Your guidance. I thank You for being my ever-present help.

Amen.

❈ FAITH IN ACTION

Write down your A, B, C, and D plans. List the names of at least three people you can ask to serve as your Plan B.

Write out three ways you can be a better employee, keeping in mind the accolades "star performers" in your workplace have received.

❆ BETWEEN FRIENDS

1. Describe a scenario in which you felt uncomfortable with praise. Ask your friends what you might have done differently.

2. Discuss any stereotypes you've run into as working moms, then talk about the various ways you can combat those prejudices by being "consummate professionals."

Set Goals for Success

*A sterling reputation is better than striking it rich; a
gracious spirit is better than money in the bank.*

—PROVERBS 22:1

The alarm clock finally beeped. Laurel looked at the time and
turned it off. She really didn't need help to wake up this morning.
She had been tossing, turning, and checking the clock all night
long. This was going to be the day that would shape her whole
professional career. Absolutely everything was on the line.

She got up and made herself a cup of tea, then she sat at the
kitchen counter with the new book her friend gave her. A Bible.

I'll give it a try, she thought.

After reading (and not absorbing much) she put her head
down and prayed. "God, I really need You with me today."

She felt the presence of the Lord speaking softly to her. "I'm
always with you."

"Yeah, well, I mean I *really* need You with me."

Getting dressed, she thought about how she had started with
nothing, built a company of her own, made it hugely profitable,
and then entered into a partnership agreement with the three
men she would face at that day's meeting.

One of them had begun to relegate her to the most menial tasks of running her division of the company and had begun to speak with open disrespect to her and about her. The other two appeared to be falling in step with the ringleader. But Laurel was nobody's chump. They would find this out today.

So how did the meeting go? I'll tell you candidly: It appeared to have gone badly. It lasted from nine in the morning until after five in the evening, and she didn't even get up to take a bathroom break.

At one point, she was reduced to tears when she pointed out all she had sacrificed for the company. After all, these three men went home to their families at the end of the day; she had never married, wasn't even dating anyone, and could hear her "biological clock" pounding instead of ticking. Now her professional life was being turned upside down.

The ringleader became incensed. He went on a verbal tirade, screaming and swearing at her with foul curses. He had never before done that in plain sight of the other two partners. It was clear that this partnership could not work.

Laurel had to decide what was important—what spelled success for her. Was it letting these men, who had an entirely different set of values, run the company their way because it meant financial security for her? Or was it more important to sacrifice financially so the company could be run with integrity?

In the end, Laurel mortgaged her house and took out a loan to buy back her stake in the company. She restarted it with just one friend who was willing to work for next to nothing initially to get it going again. Eventually, with a lot of hard work, the company was successful again. (Incidentally, the Lord also worked out the problem with her biological clock. She fell in love with and married a long-time friend, and they had a baby girl.)

How Do *You* Spell Success?

How do you define success in terms of family and career? What does a healthy family look like? Perhaps something in your family's structure needs to change. Maybe there's a better way to manage your career. Or if you finished your education, maybe more options would be available to you. Perhaps you're being called to start a whole new career or take some time off from the workplace. If God has put these types of longings in your heart, He will make a way for them to happen. But the time of transition for any type of change can be tough. Change requires effort. Sometimes the effort seems so great that remaining in the same situation appears to be the most viable option. But remember this, and you can quote me: "This is not a dress rehearsal; this is your real life."

Create Goals and Aim for Success

As my dad, Benjamin Hawkins, says, "If you aim at nothing, you can count on a bull's-eye hit on nothing every time." The key to Secret 6 is to create goals that enable you to be the very best you can be. This applies to both your personal and professional life.

But where should you begin? How can you know what goals to set, whether they are right for you and your family, and whether or not your goals are attainable? A solid, sure, and firm foundation is essential to your long-term success—no matter what your goals. There is only one foundation sure enough to build your life upon: God's wisdom, providence, and direction will be crucial to setting goals and reaching your God-given potential. Did you know there are biblical precedents to proper planning? Here's what Jesus had to say about the subject:

"Is there anyone here who, planning to build a new house, doesn't first sit down and figure the cost so you'll know if you can complete it? If you only get the foundation laid and then run out of money, you're going to look pretty foolish. Everyone passing by will poke fun at you: 'He started something he couldn't finish.'" (Luke 14:28-30)

"These words I speak to you are not mere additions to your life, homeowner improvements to your standard of living. They are foundation words, words to build a life on. If you work the words into your life, you are like a smart carpenter who dug deep and laid the foundation of his house on bedrock. When the river burst its banks and crashed against the house, nothing could shake it; it was built to last. But if you just use my words in Bible studies and don't work them into your life, you are like a dumb carpenter who built a house but skipped the foundation. When the swollen river came crashing in, it collapsed like a house of cards. It was a total loss." (Luke 6:47-49)

Prioritize and Delineate Goals

My husband, Big Dan, has had a bird's-eye view as he's watched me do the "working mom thing" for the past eight years. As a general contractor by trade, he knows a great deal about planning, organizing, and building. Ultimately, he took pity on me as I stressed over how to most clearly convey the "how-to" aspects of goal setting in this chapter. This was a blessing and a total gift from the Lord because having Dan direct his intellect toward working-mom goal setting was invaluable. (He happens to be a card-carrying member of Mensa and is a certified genius!) He came through like the cavalry with the following observations and advice:

Working moms, what are your primary goals? What objectives are nonnegotiable? The best interests of your family should obviously have top priority. God has already given you a full plate by virtue of the fact that you have children, a household to take care of, and a job. If anyone needs to prioritize and set goals within the framework of current responsibilities, it's you.

Specifically, take a look at how each activity or commitment could potentially end up creating conflicting goals. For example, accepting a promotion with higher pay might help your family financially, yet it could ultimately prove to be counterproductive if the position would take time away from your family. To avoid this conflict, establish and set values that are nonnegotiable—the things you simply cannot compromise. Your list might look something like this:

Sample Nonnegotiable Goals

- Nurture the children while equipping them for a self-sufficient future.
- See that the children achieve their potential in education.
- Ensure that they are well-adjusted at home, school, and in the community.
- Meet the physical needs of the family, keeping a roof over our heads, food on the table, and clothes on our backs.
- Maintain a good standing at work to make sure I can continue to provide for the physical and financial needs of my family.

Sample Day-to-Day Goals

- Don't start anything I can't finish.
- Finish what I start.
- Keep in mind that I barely have time to do something once. I certainly don't have time to do it a second time.

- Don't make work for myself. My aim is to be *productive*—not just busy.
- Remember that a cloud of dust and sparks flying from my heels leaves nothing but a mess for me to clean up when the dust settles.
- Be a person of accomplishment. Eradicate "what if, but if, and if only" from my mind-set.
- There's a difference between idle time and down time. Avoid idle time, and schedule down time.
- Be honest with myself about the way I am using my time. Whenever there's a time crunch, remember what's non-negotiable, then decide what I should do accordingly.

Sample Long-Range Goals

- Establish routines and rituals.
- Streamline my operations. It will make me more efficient and will actually net me time and energy.
- Lastly, don't do anything with a hard heart, resentment, or bitterness. In times of pressure, maintaining a pure heart and cheerful disposition will be almost impossible without God's help.

"Measure twice, cut once" is the carpenter's creed. I've spent more than 20 years helping people get homes and commercial real estate built, and I can attest to the fact that Jesus is right about the importance of building on a firm and solid foundation. The foundation, plan, and execution are the most important aspects of building anything that will last—including your life. So plan out your goals carefully, keeping your priorities in mind throughout the process.

In parting, I'd like to remind working moms that work can be good. God Himself worked six days when creating the earth and rested on the seventh day. As a member of the human race, you are created in the image and likeness of

God, so don't let your workload or guilt over your human limitations make things harder for you than they already are.

Don't you just love him? I certainly do.

By now, you can probably guess the first thing you should do before you set your goals: *Pray.* When you pray first, you can be clear about the direction in which God is leading you. Ask your prayer partners to pray for you, and ask your mentors to tell you what they think your strongest attributes are. When you seek the counsel of other godly women, you will gain perspective and direction on how to best live out your goals.

Dreams Versus Goals

You may already have a dream, wish, or vision for what you would like your life to be. Dreams, wishes, and vision are important, but never confuse them with goals. Wishes are stagnant. You can dream until the cows come home without making a single stride toward actualizing what you want.

Many people fall prey to staying too long in the wishing, dreaming, and imagining phase of fulfilling their God-given destiny. It is far more purposeful if you start by listening for God's leading in your life. After all, He designed you, and He has much greater perspective and a clearer vision for your destiny.

When you set your goals, they must be specific and measurable, and they should have clearly delineated steps to quantify your progress.

For example, a mother of very young children might start with the following declaration: "I will spend more quality time with my family." This is a nice wish. Even if she can imagine clearly what she would do with this quality time, it is still not a goal until it gets more specific.

"Spend one hour a day, five days per week reading or coloring with the children." This is a clear image of what she wants to do. There is even a measurable time frame included. But it still doesn't qualify as a goal. It's really just wishful thinking until she includes the steps to make it actually happen.

"Starting today, spend the hour between dinner and bedtime reading or coloring with the children instead of washing dishes. I will wash dishes after the children are already in bed from now on."

Aha! That's a goal.

Here's some further wisdom from my father, Benjamin Hawkins: "When you have no idea where you're going, you're guaranteed to get there." You don't have to end up going nowhere personally or professionally. Define what success means to you, then plan ahead and set your goals.

❋ PRAYER

Lord,

I pray You will bless me with ears to hear the sound of opportunity knocking. I ask You to give me the courage to open the door, and the stamina to walk through, even when it's difficult.

It's my heart's desire to be successful at home and at work. Let me define success by Your standards, not by the standards of the outside world, my friends, relatives, or strangers on the street. I want to follow Your perfect plan for me. Help me to know what it is.

I confess it has been hard for me to know Your will, let alone live according to it. So many voices compete for my time, telling me to turn away from Your plan. At times I feel powerless to make a decision to follow You, Lord.

It has been said that if I'll take the first step, You'll take the second, third, and fourth steps, and when I look back on my journey, I'll realize it was You who took the first step too!

Let it be so with setting new goals for my future. Bless me with a constant sense of Your presence. I thank You and I praise You with all of my heart, mind, and strength.

Amen.

❀ Faith In Action

What was the first thing to come to mind regarding setting a goal for your professional life?

What was the first thing to come to mind regarding setting a goal for your personal life?

What will you need realistically to accomplish these goals? (For example, additional education for your professional life or setting up a savings account for your personal life.)

❋ BETWEEN FRIENDS

1. What do your friends say are your strongest attributes?

2. What would you do if you could choose to do anything? What would you be?

Replenish Your Body, Mind, and Spirit

Are you tired? Worn out? Burned out on religion?
Come to me. Get away with me and you'll recover
your life. I'll show you how to take a real rest.
—MATTHEW 11:28

"Sabrina, your idea for a book sounds great. Just make sure you put something in there about getting enough sleep. I go to bed tired and I wake up tired. There has to be a solution."

This is the number-one reason women send me e-mail. Working moms say they are tired. They describe overwhelming, all-encompassing, mind-numbing fatigue in body, mind, and spirit. Most don't remember what it was like to have energy.

REST, GOD'S GIFT

If you went a day without sleep, you'd be tired, but you could probably function. What about two days? Three days? By the third day you know you would function at a reduced capacity— if you could function at all. Most of us wouldn't purposely go 72 hours without resting, but how many working moms work seven days a week? Take a moment to think about how many hours you actually work. Add up the hours you spend at your job, commuting, running errands, grocery shopping, taking the kids here and there, cooking and cleaning, doing laundry and yard work, and all the other things that have to be done to keep a family running smoothly. Are you surprised at how many hours you *really* work?

Did you know that God, the Designer of the human body (including your human body), says you are not designed to go more than six days without rest from work? "Work six days and do everything you need to do. But the seventh day is a Sabbath to GOD, your God. Don't do any work—not you, nor your son, nor your daughter, nor your servant, nor your maid, nor your animals, not even the foreign guest visiting in your town" (Exodus 20:9-10). Yep, it's right there in the Ten Commandments—the fourth commandment. It must be pretty important if God saw fit to make it one of the Ten Commandments.

Habitually breaking the fourth commandment may be the reason for much of your fatigue. It is not possible to violate a commandment from God without incurring repercussions. Every commandment is for your own good.

God designed you to operate at optimum efficiency when you take a day *every week* to rest and worship Him. When you're rejuvenated, reenergized, and refocused, you can accomplish more in six days than when you're dog-tired and sluggish for seven.

I learned this the hard way, as usual. One of my mentors, Yvonne Levy, eventually called me to task about it. After listening to me rant about the impossibility of all I had to do, she broke in with the last thing I expected to hear from another full-time working mother: "No wonder you're so tired and can't get everything done. You don't take a *Shabbat*."

A *Shabbat*? "I *know* you're not talking about a Sabbath rest!" I said, scoffing at the idea of lying around all day when I was always so far behind in housework. "You've got to be kidding me, Yvonne."

No, she wasn't kidding. She knows and lives by the Torah (the first five books of the Old Testament).

What Do You Consider Work?

As a working mom, you may have thought catching up on laundry, cleaning, bill paying, and shopping on your day off is not real work. But you are mistaken. It is probably harder work than the job you do for pay. You might think you "have" to break the fourth commandment—there simply isn't any other time available to do everything you need to do. But God will make a way for His commandment to be kept.

How? Start with prayer. I'm completely serious. Ask God to forgive you for trying to accomplish everything by human strength. Working 24/7/365 reveals a deep distrust in God's ability to see to the needs of your family.

Next, go to your children and ask them to forgive you for the times you have required them to do chores on what should have been a day of rest. I'm sure you can imagine how overjoyed my children were to hear there would be no more chores on Sundays in our family. Unexpected insight resulted from the conversation with my oldest about this. He asked if I had known all along that God didn't want us to work every day. I truthfully confessed I'd known it, but I thought I had a good reason not to follow that rule. My son looked me straight in the eyes and said, "Mommy, how could you ever think you had a good reason to disobey God?" Out of the mouths of babes . . .

Yvonne's wisdom was a real blessing for my family. And she

told me the way to make the idea of Sabbath rest into a reality: "You must prepare for the Sabbath rest the day before."

The Results

Since we instituted the Sabbath rest in our home, our kids do their housework, clean up their rooms, and put clothes away without grumbling before bedtime on Saturday night because they know that on Sunday they won't even be required to make their beds! And the Lord blesses us with supernatural energy and efficiency when preparing for a day of rest. Somehow 45 minutes of cleaning to prepare for rest accomplishes so much more than 45 minutes of cleaning dedicated to catching up. This is just another small blessing to be thankful for.

We spend Sunday mornings worshiping the Lord with people we love and who love us. Occasionally we visit friends or shut-ins, but eventually we return home to our clean and orderly house.

You can't imagine how it will revitalize you and refresh your spirit to return home and have no immediate housework looming over your head. The dishes are washed, the kids' rooms are straightened, there are no toys on the floor, and there's food in the fridge. Feel free to sit on the couch, read a book, and maybe even take a nap. God says you deserve this, He requires it, and furthermore, you need it! Not to mention it's good for your family.

As a mother who works both inside and outside the home, the temptation to burn the candle at both ends will always be tremendous. But no busy person can afford to indulge this particular besetting sin. As the old saying goes, "If you've got only six hours to cut down a tree, you'd better spend some time keeping your ax sharp." You've simply got too much to do to waste time working with a dull ax!

Use the Sample To-Do List on www.workingmom.com. It

will help you organize your days in such a way that things get done so you can have a day of rest.

SLEEP

There's probably another very good reason why you are so tired. Simply put, if you're like most working moms, you don't get enough sleep. Think about how much sleep you actually get each night. If you crawl into bed at 11:00 or later, what kind of shape are you going to be in when the alarm clock goes off just a few hours later? Even if you fall asleep within an hour of turning in, when your alarm goes off at 6:00 A.M. you've slept for only six hours. That's 25 percent less sleep than most doctors recommend! When you net only six hours of sleep per night, then you start your day only three-quarters rejuvenated. (No wonder people drink so much coffee these days!)

Stop for a moment and consider all of your responsibilities. Just being somebody's mother is a full-time job. Now add to that keeping up a home and doing a job in the paid workforce. The last person on earth who should deliberately start out behind the eight ball should be a working mom. You need more rest than anybody else because you've got more to do when you're awake!

It may sound obvious, but I'll say it anyway: Get sufficient sleep by going to bed earlier! Don't tell yourself that watching TV at night helps you unwind. Television will keep you awake until you literally crash. If you really need to unwind, reading would help you do that better than the news or a sitcom.

I suggest that you try a short-story collection instead of a full-fledged book at bedtime. You can start and finish an entire story in the span of five to 10 minutes, putting the book down with a sense of accomplishment. Take a look at www.workingmom.com for recommendations for good short-story collections. Magazines make great bedtime reading material too.

SEE YOUR DOCTOR

I'm not a doctor or a nurse, but let me advise you to see one because there's the possibility that your fatigue could be exacerbated by an underlying medical condition. For example, when I was a teenager, my parents noticed that I slept a lot. Initially, they thought it was because I was staying up too late at night talking on the phone. They also assumed that it was just a part of being a teenager. Both assumptions were partly correct. But after one particularly difficult morning, my mother declared that she was going to take me to the doctor if I was *that* tired.

She made good on the threat and took me in to see the pediatrician, who checked me out and ran a series of blood tests. When the results came back, she called my mother. "Your daughter is very anemic. She needs to start taking iron supplements right away. I'm also going to try to figure out what's causing her anemia."

The pediatrician got together with my parents' doctors and checked their medical histories. They found that my mother had the trait for sickle-cell anemia. The trait for sickle-cell is a harmless condition some people are born with. It makes them less likely to catch malaria, but more likely to be low on iron in their bloodstream (also known as anemia). Tests showed that I *did* have the trait for sickle-cell, like my mother, which explained my fatigue. After taking the iron supplements, I began to feel better.

We never would have figured out what was causing my fatigue if my parents hadn't taken me to the doctor. We could have blamed the phone or adolescent hormones. Someone might have suggested that I was depressed or had chronic fatigue syndrome or a thyroid problem or Lyme disease. There are a host of conditions that can cause fatigue, so if you're feeling exhausted, save yourself the aggravation of imagination and go see your doctor for a yearly physical. Probably no one in your family needs it more than you.

NUTRITION AND HEALTH

Have you noticed how heavy kids' book bags are these days? It makes me tired just to look at kids carrying such a heavy burden. But we moms might be carrying an extra burden around without realizing how draining it is. You're probably thinking, *Sabrina, what are you talking about?* It's time to get personal. If you've got 20 pounds or more to lose, then they're making you tired. Everywhere you go you have the equivalent of a heavy backpack or burden on your body. To make this more relevant to moms, 20 pounds is the equivalent of 24 cans of soda. Try carrying a case of sodas up a flight of stairs and you'll get the idea of what a drain 15 or 20 extra pounds are!

I'm not telling you anything you probably haven't already figured out for yourself. At least you've figured out that you've put on some extra weight. But maybe you haven't thought about how much of a strain that's putting on your energy level. I've been there too. In fact, after the birth of my second child, Christiana, I tipped the scale at a whopping 200 pounds. Okay, if I took off my watch, jewelry, hairclip, clothes, and exhaled, I was 199.5 pounds.

If I were over six feet tall, I might have looked fine. But I'm not anywhere near six feet, so it didn't look good on me and it wasn't a healthy weight for someone my height. In the weeks that followed my daughter's birth, I slimmed down to 167 pounds, and sort of leveled off at a size 16. But I could squeeze into a 12 if it was cut "right." And squeeze is exactly what I did.

My weight problem inadvertently led to my participation in the Mrs. America pageant—and it didn't happen the way you might think.

How It Really Happened

I was at a sales training meeting, and during a break I mentioned to some colleagues that I was thinking about writing a book for working moms. They said it sounded like a great idea. At the end of the conversation, I joked, "Bet you if I were Mrs. America my book would just fly off the shelves!" We all laughed and I thought that was the end of it.

It wasn't.

Have you ever been made to feel like a fool? Of course you have. And that's exactly what happened to yours truly when one of the ladies who was part of the conversation said to the rest of our group, "Sabrina, why don't you tell everyone about your idea?"

Naturally, I thought she was talking about the book, and I started going over some of my ideas. She interrupted me with the smuggest look I've ever seen on the face of a human being: "Not your book. Tell them about your plan to be in the Mrs. America Pageant."

Now, believe me when I say that you had to be there. This was not a simple misunderstanding. It was meant to make fun of me. You see, at that point in my life, I had my hair in dreadlocks, had never plucked my eyebrows—EVER—and I definitely needed to lose some weight.

The rest of the group began to chime in, "You can do it! Why not? You're attractive!" They were all just being polite. I could tell they were all thinking, *She's not bad looking, but I can't believe she thinks she's a beauty queen!* The more I protested, the more they felt obligated to tell me to go for it.

In tears, I called my husband during the next break. This is rare for me, because I'm not one to cry often. I told him the whole story and how I wanted to quit my job because I couldn't face everyone.

Inspiration from Big Dan

In one of those moments when a husband says the right thing, Dan came out with this: "You know, if a guy didn't like you, he would just say so. But women—women can be *evil!* She picked the wrong woman this time, because you're the prettiest girl I've ever seen in my whole life."

"Well, you just think I'm pretty because I'm your wife," I whimpered, ever so slightly placated by his compliment.

"I'll tell you what we're going to do," Dan continued. "We'll go over to your parents' house, log onto the Internet, and find out what you have to do to be Mrs. America."

Thus began my foray into the arena of modern-day pageantry. The company I worked for sponsored me with media training, and introduced me to the press. Lenox China (which is made in New Jersey) sponsored me by providing gifts for the contestants in the pageant. The place where I had bought my prom dress more than 10 years before sponsored me with gowns and interview suits. Ellen Lange Skin Science, owned by the sister of one of my high school friends, sponsored me with weekly facials and microdermabrasion treatments. And my dentist's office took out all my gray amalgam fillings, replaced them with white ones, and whitened my teeth. You should see me when I laugh with my mouth open—fabulous!

The pressure was on, and I knew I had to get in shape quickly. I had seven months to lose 42 pounds. Incidentally, even though there's no weight restriction in the Mrs. New Jersey or Mrs. America Pageant, I didn't intend to get up there out of shape.

Losing Weight, Shaping Up

Here's how I lost the weight, and it was ridiculously simple—though the first three days weren't easy. I kept eating everything I normally would eat, but I simply stopped eating sweets, excessive pasta, rice, bread, and chips. I filled up on salads, lean meats, and seafood, and I drank water instead of sodas and juices. For snacks, I ate strawberries sweetened with Splenda. My weight melted off.

Now let me say this: I suggest you speak to your doctor or a dietician before implementing any new diet or exercise plan. After all, just because something worked for me, doesn't necessarily mean that it's right for you.

I'll tell you the truth: The first three days of giving up the sweets and high starch foods were just about unbearable. Everywhere I looked there was a donut shop or bakery. I could spot them a mile away from my moving vehicle. Honestly, sweets and starches called out to me like there was no tomorrow. After I finally made it past the third day, though, the cravings went away.

There's another thing you should know: A skinny girl can have a protruding tummy, and mushy, jiggly arms and legs. The reason I know is because it happened to me. (And it looks as unsightly as it sounds.) With the help of trainers at my gym, I toned up my long-neglected muscles by lifting weights. In less than three months I had pretty impressive muscle tone.

But the best part of losing the weight and increasing my muscle mass was the phenomenal physical energy I gained! You won't believe how much pep you can put in your step when you're in good shape.

Your Challenge

Because of a working mom's time constraints, there are unique challenges to diet and exercise. Most of us don't have the time for traditional exercise programs, nor can we always fit in balanced, nutritious meals. But if you watch the sugars, starches, and junk food and make a commitment to work out with weights for a half hour five days a week until you hit your goal, victory can be yours.

If you don't have time to hit the gym or you don't want to take more time away from your family, try this: Buy some hand weights, an exercise ball, and a couple of short exercise DVDs, and exercise at home. (I recommend the shorter programs because you may become discouraged and quit if you can't find time for an entire hour of exercise.) Finally, get your husband and kids involved in your fitness program. Take walks or bike rides together. Get the kids to do the exercise DVD with you. Make getting in shape a family affair; husbands and kids need exercise too!

Some encouragement to keep in mind is this: After you achieve your fitness goal, maintenance is much, much easier. I can have an occasional sweet treat, and now I need to work out only once or twice a week to stay in shape.

When you employ reality-based approaches, success is assured. The keys to reducing exhaustion are getting an annual physical to address any underlying health issues, getting sufficient sleep, taking a day off from working, maintaining the right diet, and increasing muscle tone and fitness through exercise.

REPLENISHING YOUR SPIRIT

I've already talked about spiritual replenishment in other chapters, so I'll just remind you here that replenishing your spirit is every bit as important as replenishing your body and mind. Reading and meditating on God's Word, worshiping with friends and family, praying for others and having them pray for you, taking a Sabbath rest each week, singing songs of praise—these are all important to your spiritual health. If you've been ignoring this aspect of your being, I hope you'll be encouraged to begin at least one or two spiritual practices. Try it. It will make a big difference in your life.

❋ PRAYER

Lord,

   Renew me. Replenish my body, mind, and spirit. Enable me to soar. Make my heart and countenance light. Surround me with the sense of Your presence. Give me a thirst for You, Your Word, and Your people. Keep me forever in the center of Your will.

   Give me the resolve to follow You all the days of my life. Bless my family that they may follow after You too. I'm onto something bigger than I can grasp. That's why I come before You asking You to hold on to me. I don't have the power to hold on to You.

   I love You, Lord Jesus. Thank You for saving me. I praise You, worship You, and adore You. You are like no other person who ever lived. The whole world measures time by Your coming, and the years after Your arrival (B.C. and A.D.). Help me to remember that You are the Lord of everything, and even time itself is subject to Your authority.

   I ask that You hear my prayer in the name of my Lord and Savior Jesus Christ.

   Amen.

❀ FAITH IN ACTION

What three or four changes do you want to make as a result of reading this book? List them.

Who can you speak to for help in becoming the woman you desire to be?

When would be the best time for you to read and study your Bible? Make a commitment to set aside time each day to replenish your spirit.

✳ BETWEEN FRIENDS

1. What challenges do you need to overcome to eat a more balanced diet, exercise, and get more rest?

2. How can your friends help you reach your goals?

3. In what ways have you been neglecting your spiritual health? What one change can you make in that area?

Epilogue

The New Typical Morning

Look at the nations and watch—and be utterly amazed. For I am going to do something in your days that you would not believe, even if you were told.
—HABAKKUK 1:5, NIV

6:15 A.M.—The alarm clock rings.

6:16—You wake up and smell the coffee.

6:20—Sitting at the kitchen table with a Bible and morning devotional, you pray for your family, your friends, and your upcoming day.

6:40—Into the bathroom you go, multitasking shaving your legs while the shower warms up and you brush your teeth.

7:00—Your makeup is on, your hair is done; you are dressed and ready.

7:05—You wake up the kids gently with a rub on the back and a soft song. You open the shades and declare with sincerity, "Rise and shine! It's a beautiful day and you don't want to miss it!"

7:30—The family has breakfast together. Thanks to the microwave and precooked bacon, you can make bacon, egg, and cheese sandwiches in less than three minutes.

7:45—You give the kids lunch money instead of packing lunch.

7:48—You permit them to play with their toys after clearing their dishes from the table.

7:49—With a glance at your to-do list, you take meat out of the freezer.

7:53—The breakfast dishes are done. The kids' book bags and your purse are at the door, ready to go.

8:00—The kids put on jackets and caps and wait for the bus. You pray for the Lord's protection and providence over them.

8:03—The bus arrives.

8:05—While driving to work, you call one of your prayer partners using your "hands-free" cell phone just to check in and let her know you care.

8:15—You arrive at work with 15 minutes to spare. You get a jump-start on your work, making great progress during the quiet time.

8:29—The boss walks in and finds you already hard at work. He comments, "I wish I had a dozen more employees like you!"

8:30—You respond graciously, "Thank you. I appreciate the compliment."

This promises to be an enriching day. Your family's morning was calm and peaceful. Everyone's needs were met. You, Working Mom, have a stellar reputation at work, and nothing is too hard to handle. Even if a child had been unable to go to school, there was a reliable contingency plan.

You have a personal relationship with God, and you have prayer partners. You have eliminated extraneous commitments, you delegate appropriately, and you multitask the rest. You show up big time at work and have your goals for success in sight. You are healthy and rested. You never let your spirit run dry, because you regularly drink from the wellspring of life through Jesus Christ.

What was once just a dream is now your typical morning.

Appendix 1

Making the Decision to Work Outside the Home

From time to time, every mom needs to reevaluate whether to work as her children's needs change. God may call you to be at home for a certain season of your children's growing-up years. If so, make chronological *and* financial plans for your transition from the workplace to the home before making a change. Here are a few tips that will help in making this decision:

- Pray about whether working outside the home is God's will for you at this time.
- Keep the bottom line of your decision this: "What's best for my kids?" As much as you might love your job or income, you love your children more. Their best interests should always be top priority.
- Do a careful financial analysis. To start with, be sure your current income brings in an actual financial benefit for your family. Take into account the increased tax bracket, the cost of commuting, childcare, wardrobe, lunches out, and so on. In some cases the benefits of working may not be as significant as you might have thought. I recommend Mary Larmoyeux's book *There's No Place Like Home* and Larry Burkett's *Women Leaving the Workplace* for further guidance on how others have successfully made the transition.

- Finally, if you've addressed all these points, and your husband does not support the idea of your leaving the workplace or the numbers still don't add up, then don't worry, feel guilty, or stress about it. God very well may be calling you to continue working outside the home for the time being. Continue to pray, live frugally, and maintain a cheerful disposition. As long as the needs of your family are being met, work heartily as unto the Lord and work in the freedom of His grace!

Appendix 2

Great Time-Savers for Families

Working Mom™ Household Job Chart
Working Mom™ Fast Fax Grocery List
Baby-Sitter Checklist

For other great time-savers go to
www.workingmom.com!

*Working Mom™ Household Job Chart**

3- to 4-YEAR-OLDS CAN:
___ Pick up toys
___ Fold dishtowels and washcloths
___ Match socks
___ Put small items in the garbage
___ Give food to pets
___ Water indoor plants

5- to 6-YEAR-OLDS CAN ALSO:
___ Answer the telephone
___ Sweep a deck/patio/porch
___ Wipe the bathroom sink
___ Put forks and spoons away
___ Put their own clothes in the drawer
___ Sort laundry into color piles
___ Use a hand-held vacuum

7- to 9-YEAR-OLDS CAN ALSO:
___ Take out garbage
___ Set the table
___ Clear the table
___ Vacuum an area rug
___ Clean the inside of the car
___ Empty the dishwasher
___ Water the garden

10- to 12-YEAR-OLDS CAN ALSO:

___ Clean mirrors

___ Clean kitchen counters and sink

___ Fold and put away laundry

___ Put away groceries

___ Pack their own lunch

___ Do light yard work

___ Load the dishwasher

13- to 14-YEAR-OLDS CAN ALSO:

___ Clean the bathroom

___ Change bed sheets

___ Mow the lawn

___ Wash dishes by hand

___ Wash the car

___ Do laundry

___ Shovel snow

15 YEARS AND UP CAN ALSO:

___ Use a leafblower

___ Use a snowblower

___ Clean the refrigerator

___ Reorganize storage areas

___ Make dinner

*Ages listed are approximate, and capabilities will vary depending on the individual child.

Working Mom™ *Fast-Fax Grocery List*

STAPLES
- ❐ Cereal
- ❐ Grits
- ❐ Bread
- ❐ Sugar
- ❐ Buns
- ❐ _____
- ❐ _____

SPICES
- ❐ Salt/Pepper
- ❐ Bacon Bits
- ❐ Chocolate
- ❐ Seasoning
- ❐ Garlic
- ❐ _____
- ❐ _____

STARCHES
- ❐ Potato Mix
- ❐ Rice
- ❐ Spaghetti
- ❐ Sauce
- ❐ _____
- ❐ _____

DRINKS
- ❐ Apple
- ❐ Soda
- ❐ Juice Boxes
- ❐ Water Filters

- ❐ Coffee
- ❐ Decaf
- ❐ Tea
- ❐ Orange
- ❐ Cranberry
- ❐ Grape
- ❐ _____
- ❐ _____

CANNED
- ❐ Olives
- ❐ Soups
- ❐ Beans
- ❐ Tuna
- ❐ _____
- ❐ _____

CONDIMENTS
- ❐ Ketchup
- ❐ Jelly
- ❐ Peanut Butter
- ❐ Mayonnaise
- ❐ Olive Oil
- ❐ Salad Dressing
- ❐ _____
- ❐ _____

PAPER
- ❐ Napkins
- ❐ Plates
- ❐ Cups

- ❐ Paper Towels
- ❐ Aluminum Foil
- ❐ Toilet Paper
- ❐ Garbage Bag
- ❐ Zip Locks
- ❐ _____
- ❐ _____

CLEANING
- ❐ Bleach
- ❐ Detergent
- ❐ Dish Liquid
- ❐ Dishwasher Tabs
- ❐ Fabric Softener
- ❐ Light Bulbs
- ❐ Vacuum Bags
- ❐ Cleaning Wipes
- ❐ Bathroom Foam
- ❐ Window Cleaner
- ❐ _____
- ❐ _____

MEATS
- ❐ Beef
- ❐ Chicken
- ❐ Turkey
- ❐ Fish
- ❐ Bacon
- ❐ Sausage
- ❐ _____
- ❐ _____

PRODUCE
- ❏ Apples
- ❏ Oranges
- ❏ Bananas
- ❏ Strawberries
- ❏ Mangos
- ❏ Lettuce
- ❏ Celery
- ❏ Cucumbers
- ❏ Tomatoes
- ❏ _____
- ❏ _____

PERSONAL
- ❏ Soap
- ❏ Shampoo
- ❏ Conditioner
- ❏ Detangler
- ❏ Barrettes
- ❏ Lip Balm
- ❏ Lotion
- ❏ Pads/Tampons
- ❏ _____
- ❏ _____

FROZEN
- ❏ Broccoli
- ❏ Green Beans
- ❏ Peas
- ❏ Corn
- ❏ Mixed Vegetables
- ❏ Ice Cream
- ❏ Fish Sticks
- ❏ Nuggets
- ❏ _____
- ❏ _____

DAIRY
- ❏ Milk
- ❏ Butter
- ❏ Cheese
- ❏ Eggs
- ❏ Creamer
- ❏ Yogurt
- ❏ _____
- ❏ _____

BABY
- ❏ Diapers

- ❏ Wipes
- ❏ Baby Food
- ❏ Formula
- ❏ _____
- ❏ _____

MISC.
- ❏ _____
- ❏ _____
- ❏ _____
- ❏ _____
- ❏ _____
- ❏ _____
- ❏ _____
- ❏ _____
- ❏ _____
- ❏ _____
- ❏ _____
- ❏ _____
- ❏ _____
- ❏ _____
- ❏ _____
- ❏ _____
- ❏ _____

Baby-Sitter Checklist

Where I'll be: _____

Phone # there: _____   I'll be back at: _____

If I can't be reached, call

My Cell: _____

Name: _____   Phone: _____

Important Information

Police: _____

This address: _____

Nearest cross street: _____

Insurance: _____   Policy #: _____

House Keys are: _____   Car Keys are: _____

Garage Remote: _____

About the Child(ren)

Name/s: _____   _____   _____

Age/s: _____

Weight: _____   Height: _____

Medications: _____

Allergies: _____

Bedtime: _____

Other Information: _____

* PERMISSION IS GRANTED: Any licensed physician, dentist, or hospital may give necessary emergency medical service to my child at the request of the person bearing this form with note to the allergies, medications, and other information listed above.

Signed: _____
                    (parent/guardian)

Date: _____

Acknowledgments

God the Father, Jesus the Son, and the Holy Spirit—Thank You for blessing the work of my hands and for this consuming passion to reach the lost. But most of all, thank You for our relationship. Thank You for saving me, teaching me, opening my eyes, healing my hurts, and pouring out Your love, grace, and mercy on me. Using me to share with others is humbling. You're simply magnificent.

Daniel—The man who rocked my world. Sharing your name and sharing your life have been the greatest adventure. Fifteen years later, it's still a thrill to say, "That's *my man!*"

Daniel, Christiana, and Angelica—My children. You are truly blessings. This book wouldn't have been possible without your patience while "Mama's writin' Workin' Mom."

Calvin and Benjamin Hawkins—My parents. God has used you greatly to pour out His wisdom and love. Thank you for investing so much in me. I love you.

David Van Diest—The Working Mom™ crowbar. The Lord has used you to open doors that were nailed shut. You are the best of the best; no other literary agent comes close.

Janis Long Harris—You've consistently blazed trails in "no-woman's land." Because of you, working moms have footsteps to follow. Thank you.

About Working Mom™

Working Mom™ is an evangelical part of the universal Christian church. Its message is based on the Bible. Its ministry is motivated by the love of God. Its mission is to show the love of Jesus Christ and to provide help in His name without discrimination. We address both the practical and spiritual needs of families with a mom in the workforce.

"Saving Time, Energy, and Money"
is the Working Mom™ motto.

"Revitalizing the Working Mom™" is our mission.

"Replenishing the Working Mom's Spirit" is our purpose.

Our Web site, WorkingMom.com, is visited primarily by people without a religious background. We've shattered stereotypes about working mothers and religious people, as well as businesswomen. We hope and pray that the readers of *Moms on the Job* will stop by our Web site, get encouraged, inspired, and pick up some free timesaving tools and instant online grocery coupons to become better equipped to overcome the challenges of being a busy working mom.

Working Mom™
424 Park Avenue South
Suite 200
New York, NY 10016-8010
(212) 772 -9377

FREE Discussion Guide!
A discussion guide for Moms on the Job is available at
ChristianBookGuides.com

FOCUS ON THE FAMILY®

Welcome to the family!

Whether you purchased this book, borrowed it, or received it as a gift, we're glad you're reading it. It's just one of the many helpful, encouraging, and biblically based resources produced by Focus on the Family for people in all stages of life.

Focus began in 1977 with the vision of one man, Dr. James Dobson, a licensed psychologist and author of numerous best-selling books on marriage, parenting, and family. Alarmed by the societal, political, and economic pressures that were threatening the existence of the American family, Dr. Dobson founded Focus on the Family with one employee and a once-a-week radio broadcast aired on 36 stations.

Now an international organization reaching millions of people daily, Focus on the Family is dedicated to preserving values and strengthening and encouraging families through the life-changing message of Jesus Christ.

Focus on the Family Magazines

These faith-building, character-developing publications address the interests, issues, concerns, and challenges faced by every member of your family from preschool through the senior years.

| Focus on the Family **Citizen®** U.S. news issues | Focus on the Family **Clubhouse Jr.™** Ages 4 to 8 | Focus on the Family **Clubhouse™** Ages 8 to 12 | **Breakaway®** Teen guys | **Brio®** Teen girls 12 to 16 | **Brio & Beyond®** Teen girls 16 to 19 | **Plugged In®** Reviews movies, music, TV |

FOR MORE INFORMATION

Online:
Log on to www.family.org.
In Canada, log on to www.focusonthefamily.ca.

Phone:
Call toll free: (800) A-FAMILY (232-6459).
In Canada, call toll free: (800) 661-9800.

more **great resources**
from Focus on the Family®

Blessing Your Husband

In *Blessing Your Husband*, Debra Evans brings wise scriptural insights and true stories of what happens when a wife chooses to make blessing her husband a priority. By understanding a husband's unique characteristics, how he thinks, and what matters most to him, each wife can affirm her mate and develop a closer, more satisfying relationship. Hardcover.

Parenting at the Speed of Life

This fresh, encouraging, and empowering book will show you unique opportunities to connect with your kids in the ordinary moments of each day — no supplies or creativity needed! Life may be hectic, but you can learn how to bless your children in mere minutes and impact your kids' lives for tomorrow! Paperback.

Your Child DVD Parenting Seminar: Home Edition

Essentials of Discipline tackles the subject of discipline in a way that only Dr. James Dobson can. Based on his time-tested best sellers, you know the content has substance, but this video seminar also includes animation and man-on-the-street interviews. Lessons from Dr. Dobson have never been this fun! Three DVDs and parent's guide.